INDEPENDENCE AND REVOLUTION IN

M E X I C O

1810–1940

WORLD HISTORY LIBRARY

INDEPENDENCE AND REVOLUTION IN
MEXICO
1810 – 1940

REBECCA STEFOFF

Facts On File

On the cover: Emiliano Zapata, by Diego Rivera, 1930

Independence and Revolution in Mexico, 1810–1940

Facts On File, Inc.
460 Park Avenue South
New York NY 10016

Library of Congress Cataloging-in-Publication Data
Stefoff, Rebecca, 1951-
    Independence and revolution in Mexico : 1810–1940 / Rebecca Stefoff.
    p.   cm. — (World history library)
    Includes bibliographical references and index.
    Summary: Examines the most turbulent period in Mexican history and the revolutions that were instrumental in bringing about independence from Spain, the loss of American colonies, and other political changes.
    ISBN 0-8160-2841-9 (alk. paper)
    1. Mexico—History—1810- —Juvenile literature. [1. Mexico—History—1810-] I. Title. II. Series.
F1208.5.S72   1993
972—dc20   92-37380

A British CIP catalogue record for this book is available from the British Library.

Facts On File books are available at special discounts when purchased in bulk quantities for businesses, associations, institutions or sales promotions. Please contact our Special Sales Department in New York at 212/683-2244, 800/322-8755.

Text design by Donna Sinisgalli
Cover design by Amy Gonzalez
Composition by Facts On File, Inc./Robert Yaffe
Manufactured by the Maple-Vail Book Manufacturing Group
Printed in the United States of America

10 9 8 7 6 5 4 3 2 1

This book is printed on acid-free paper.

CONTENTS

*Any people can be free
that wants to be.*

—Father Miguel Hidalgo y Costilla, 1810

Mexicali

BAJA CALIFORNIA NORTE

Tucson

El Paso

Nogales
Agua Prieta
Ciudad Juárez (formerly El Paso del Norte)

Cananea

Río Grande

SONORA

Casas Grandes

Hermosillo

CHIHUAHUA

Chihuahua

Guaymas
Navojoa

Camargo

COAH

Gulf of California

Jiménez

Cuatrocié

BAJA CALIFORNIA SUR

Los Mochis
Sinaloa

Gómez Palacio
Torre

Culiacán

SINALOA

DURANGO

Pacific Ocean

La Paz

Durango

ZACAT

Mazatlán

Fresnillo

NAYARIT

Zaca

AGUASCALI

San Blas

Tepic

Guadalajara

Mexico

Atotonilco

JALISCO
Tuxpan

Colima

Apatzing

Manzanillo

MICHOAC

Miles

0   100   200   300

● Major Cities
O State Capitals
✪ National Capital

Mexico City Area

VERACRUZ

Dolores Hidalgo

San Miguel

Guanajuato
○ Guanajuato
GUANAJUATO ○ QUERÉTARO

● Querétaro

HIDALGO

Celaya

MICHOACÁN **MEXICO**
○
Morelia Mexico **TLAXCALA**
(formerly City
Valladolid) Toluca ○ ● Puebla
○ Cuernavaca
● Cuautla
MORELOS **PUEBLA**

Miles (inset)

0   100

edras Negras
ormerly Ciudad Porfirio Díaz)

○va ● Nuevo Laredo

JEVO
EÓN
terrey
○

Reynosa
● Matamoros

Ciudad
Victoria
○
TAMAULIPAS

LUIS
OSÍ
Luis Potosí

● Tampico

**Gulf of
Mexico**

*see
inset*

Mexico
City ◉

guala ●
UERRERO
○
ilpancingo
capulco

○ Jalapa
● Veracruz

● Córdoba
Villahermosa
○
VERACRUZ   **TABASCO** ○

Oaxaca ○

Tuxtla
Gutiérrez **CHIAPAS**
○
● San Cristobal
de las Casas
OAXACA
● Tonalá

Progreso
●
Yucatán ○ Mérida Cozumel
Peninsula **YUCATÁN** ●

QUINTANA ROO

Campeche ○

CAMPECHE ○
Ciudad
Chetumal

THE LAST DAYS OF NEW SPAIN

Mexico is a land of mountains, and many of its mountains are volcanoes. The tallest of these is Pico de Orizaba, which the Aztecs called the Mountain of the Star; its snowcapped peak can be seen for a hundred miles out to sea in the Gulf of Mexico. On the country's central plateau, Popocatepetl and other volcanoes overlook Mexico City, the capital, whose residents are familiar with volcanic smokes and rumbles. For thousands of years, volcanic eruptions and the earthquakes that are associated with them have periodically unleashed destruction upon the Mexican countryside. Yet the layers of volcanic ash have also enriched the soil, making the slopes of the volcanoes and the plains around them the most fertile parts of the country.

At the beginning of the 19th century, Mexico itself was like a volcano that, after simmering and bubbling deep inside for a long time, was on the verge of an eruption. For nearly three centuries Mexico had been a Spanish colony called New Spain. Three hundred years of Spanish rule had created a Mexico that was deeply divided along class, race, and economic lines. Not only was tension rising among various groups within the colony's population, but many colonials were growing increasingly resentful of Spanish domination. More and more voices in New Spain were calling out for change.

New Spain was born in 1519, when Spanish adventurer Hernán Cortés landed on the east coast of Mexico with 555 soldiers and 16 horses. Cortés and his followers found themselves in a land with a long and rich history. Native American civilizations had flourished in Mexico for more than 2,000 years before the Spanish arrived. Peoples such as the Olmecs, Toltecs, Mixtecs, Mayas, Aztecs, and Zapotecs had developed sophisticated political and economic systems. They built large cities and massive temples, they became expert in mathematics and astronomy, and they produced master craftspeople and artisans. In Cortés's day the Aztecs were the most powerful force in Mexico, but the Spanish, equipped with muskets, steel knives and spears, armor, and warhorses—none of which had ever been seen before in the Americas—were able to conquer the mighty Aztec empire in just two years. Mexico City, the new Spanish capital, rose on the site of the old Aztec capital Tenochtitlán.

For the first few years of the conquest, Mexico remained in the hands of Cortés and his fellow conquistadores, who claimed the American territory in the name of the Spanish crown. In 1535 the crown created a formal administration for the colony, which was now called the viceroyalty of New Spain. The colony's senior official was the viceroy, who was appointed by the crown; New Spain was to be governed by a succession of viceroys until 1821. Before long, a large administrative bureaucracy sprouted in New Spain, and it continued to grow throughout the colonial era. Among the bureaucrats who ran the colony under the supervision of the viceroy were magistrates, judges, tax collectors, lawyers, royal inspectors, town councilmen, and regional officials called corregidores (officers of the crown), alcaldes (mayors), and gobernadores (governors). Some were capable and honest men, but others were greedy, incompetent, and corrupt. All too often officials filled their own pockets with taxes, bribes, and public funds at the expense of the people they were supposed to govern.

At first New Spain consisted of the east coast of Mexico, where Cortés had landed at the site of the modern city of Veracruz, and the central plateau around Mexico City, which had long been the most densely

With muskets and steel, the Spanish conquistadores seized Mexico in the 16th century. They founded an overseas empire for Spain but brought oppression and suffering to the Native American peoples they conquered. (Library of Congress)

populated part of the land. But the colony grew larger as missionaries and explorers pushed west, south, and north from the center. Soon the Spanish reached Mexico's west coast. There they built ports such as Acapulco to trade across the Pacific Ocean with the Philippine Islands, Spain's Asian colony. On Mexico's southern border the Spanish established the colony of Guatemala, which included most of present-day Central America. To the north of central Mexico lay a vast unknown expanse of rugged country, consisting mostly of mountains, gorges, deserts, and sunbaked semiarid grasslands: a region that today includes northern Mexico and the southwestern United States. As early as 1540 a Spanish conquistador named Francisco Vázquez de Coronado probed this land, seeking mythical cities of gold, and in the centuries that followed the frontier of New Spain edged ever northward. By the 1770s New Spain stretched all the way to San Francisco on the California coast and included present-day Arizona, New Mexico, Texas, and parts of several other states. At its greatest extent New Spain was twice as large as Mexico is today. But much of this territory, especially in the north, was only sparsely settled by the Spanish. The Native American population outnumbered the European population in most parts of the colony, from the steamy, low-lying Yucatán Peninsula in the southeast, home of the Maya civilization, to the dry, mountainous uplands of the northwest, peopled by roving bands of nomadic hunters.

No one knows for sure how many Indians lived in Mexico when the Spanish first arrived. In their 1963 book *The Aboriginal Population of Central Mexico on the Eve of the Spanish Conquest,* historians Sherburne F. Cook and Woodrow Borah argue that the Indian population of the central plateau alone was more than 25 million; other scholars believe that this figure is far too high. All historians agree, however, that the number of Indians dropped dramatically after the Spanish conquest, partly because many Indians were killed in the fighting, but mostly because of diseases introduced by the European newcomers. Smallpox and measles were unknown in the Americas before the conquest. Native Americans therefore had not developed natural immunities to these common European diseases, and as a result the Indians died by the millions when epidemics swept through the population. The Europeans cannot be blamed for all the epidemics, however; a plague that the Indians called *matlazahuatl,* now believed to be a form of typhus, existed in Mexico before the Spanish came, and it continued to ravage both Indian and white populations, killing 800,000 people in 1545 and 2 million in 1576.

In addition to war and disease, the Indians suffered from the treatment they received at the hands of their Spanish overlords, especially during the first century after the conquest. As their reward for conquering Mexico, the conquistadores were granted huge tracts of property called *encomiendas,* which they passed on to their descendants. The holder of an encomienda controlled not just the land but also the people who lived on it. Under the encomienda system many Indians became slaves, whose owners overworked, relocated, abused, and even killed them at will. From the start of the colony, however, both the Roman Catholic church and the Spanish crown claimed that they wanted to protect the Indians from cruelty and exploitation. The crown soon stopped granting encomiendas, and these private fiefdoms declined greatly in size, number, and influence after the 16th century. But the damage had already been done: Families, villages, and entire cultures had been broken up, thousands of unwilling laborers had been killed, and—most harmful of all—the European colonists had grown accustomed to thinking of the Indians as inferior, servile beings and treating them accordingly. This attitude lingered, poisoning relations between the races, long after the last encomiendas disappeared. And although laws were passed in Spain to improve the status of the Indians, those laws proved difficult to enforce in Mexico, where they were often ignored. Many Indians were reduced to the status of peons. They owned no land but worked as tenant laborers for the white owners of *latifundia,* large farms and ranches. The peons received only tiny wages. Often they were virtually enslaved by a crushing burden of debt, which was passed on to their children and grandchildren, who in turn were forced to work for the landowner to pay off the debt. In many ways peonage was just another form of slavery.

As a result of all these woes, by the year 1625—just a century after the Spanish conquest—the Indian population of Mexico had fallen to an all-time low of about 1 million. In the following centuries it rose slowly. And a new racial group appeared, not only in New Spain but in other Spanish colonies in Central and South America. These were the *mestizos,* the people of mixed European and Indian blood. Most of the early mestizos were the children of white fathers and Indian mothers. A few mestizos, especially those with fair skin and European features, were recognized by their fathers and given places in Spanish colonial society. But the majority of the mestizos grew up within the Indian culture and were regarded as inferiors or social outcasts by the whites. They shared this lowly status not only with pureblooded Indians but also with three other racial groups: the Africans who had been brought to Mexico as slaves, the mulattoes (people of mixed black and white descent), and the zambos (people of mixed black and Indian descent). Together these

SOR JUANA:
A WOMAN'S LOVE OF LEARNING

Colonial Mexican society did not offer much scope for women who wanted to lead independent, creative lives. Women's roles were limited to marriage and service to the church. Yet even during this repressive era one woman managed to become not only the greatest poet of New Spain but also the first great poet of the Americas.

Juana Inés de Asbaje was born in 1651 in the village of San Miguel Nepantla, not far from Mexico City. Her parents quickly became aware that their little girl was brilliant and gifted—she learned to read at the age of three and began educating herself from her grandfather's library. By the age of eight she was writing poetry and begging to be sent to the university in Mexico City. A year later she was sent to the capital to continue her studies. She learned to read and write Latin in only 20 lessons, and she continued to write witty, elegant poetry.

Soon all of Mexico City was buzzing with the news of this remarkable girl. The viceroy invited her to his court, where she became an attendant of the vicereine, the viceroy's wife. She was popular for her charm and beauty, but her admirers were most amazed by her wit and learning. When she was 17 years old, the viceroy arranged a demonstration of her knowledge. Forty professors from the university quizzed her on all sorts of subjects, and she answered all their questions not only correctly but cleverly and in stylish, polished language. She was the toast of Mexico City.

But in 1669 she put an end to her public life as a celebrity. She joined the convent of San Jeronimo and became a nun. From then on she was known as Sor Juana Inés de la Cruz (Sister Juana Inés of the Cross). Some have said that she adopted the religious life to escape the clutches of an unwanted

nonwhite groups greatly outnumbered the whites in New Spain. By 1810 the colony's population was made up of 3.7 million Indians, at least 2 million mestizos, 1.2 million whites, and about 6,000 people of African descent.

suitor, or perhaps in sorrow over a disappointment in love. But no romantic fantasies are needed to explain her decision—she was a born scholar, and she realized that the convent was the only place where she would be allowed to devote herself to full-time study and writing. For several decades she lived a life of great intellectual freedom. Although she was isolated from the world of action and events, she assembled a library of more than 4,000 books, she carried out scientific experiments, she mastered a variety of musical instruments, and she had many distinguished visitors.

Sor Juan also wrote many poems and plays. Some were about religious subjects, while others were about love, history, and politics. The broad range of her interests finally got her into trouble with her superiors in the church, who criticized her for being too broad-minded and worldly. She was ordered to confine herself to religious studies. In 1691 she wrote a letter to the bishop defending her way of life and her desire for knowledge. But pressure from the church authorities increased, and in 1693 Sor Juana was forced to submit. With her own blood she signed a confession stating that her passion for learning was worldly and irreligious. She sold her books and musical instruments, gave the money to the poor, and withdrew from all contact with the world to spend her time on religious duties. Two years later she died while nursing her sister nuns through an epidemic.

Sor Juana's poems have been translated into many languages and read around the world. They are written in a 17th-century style that may seem stiff and artificial to modern readers, but they deal with universal feelings and problems: the beauty of the natural world, a joyous love of God, the unfairness of society's artificial rules, and the mysterious and often troubled relations between men and women. Today Sor Juana is recognized as an important poet and also as a pioneer of women's rights, a woman who even as a small child claimed the right to a life of her own design.

Most of the white population of New Spain lived in and around the capital and other major cities. Mexico City grew steadily throughout the colonial era, outstripping all other urban centers. In the first decade of the 19th century, Mexico City was still the largest

Mexico City in the early 19th century. The Spanish built Mexico's capital city on the site of Tenochtitlán, the capital of the vanquished Aztec civilization. (Library of Congress)

city in the Western Hemisphere, with a population of 170,000. It was the educational center of Spanish America; its schools included the oldest university in the Americas (the Royal and Pontifical University of Mexico, where classes began in 1553) and a renowned college of mining and geology. Mexico City was also the cultural center of New Spain—at least, it was the heart of cultural activities in the European tradition, such as opera, the formal study of art, and book and newspaper publishing. Other arts, however, were practiced throughout the colony and soon took on a decidedly Native American cast. Spanish-style popular music was influenced by traditional Indian melodies and instruments, and Spanish-style architecture soon reflected some features of Aztec and Maya buildings, such as colored stone, flat roofs, and thick, earthquake-proof walls.

The Spanish and Indian traditions blended most richly in painting and sculpture. These arts were concerned chiefly with religious subjects. The Catholic missionaries built hundreds of churches throughout New Spain, and they trained Indian artisans to ornament the churches with paintings, murals, stone statues, and glorious wooden carvings. Many of these artists worked Native American images and symbols into their work or portrayed Christ, the Virgin Mary, and the saints with Indian faces. Some of Mexico's cathedral decorations are recognized today as masterpieces of world art.

No aspect of European civilization had a more profound or wide-ranging effect on the lives of Mexico's Indians than the Catholic church. From the first days of the conquest, the church had viewed the Native Americans as souls to be saved for Christ. The Jesuits, Franciscans, Dominicans, and other religious orders that set up missions to convert the Indians were both patient and clever. They did not try to stamp out traditional beliefs altogether. Instead they built their churches on the sites of ancient holy places and allowed the Catholic saints to take on some of the attributes of Aztec deities. They also permitted the Indian worshippers to combine elements of their traditional rituals with the Catholic festivals. This toleration won for the churchmen the fervent loyalty of the Indians and mestizos.

Not all members of the Catholic clergy were tolerant of Native American ways. A few of them burned Indian artifacts and tried to destroy all traces of a culture that they thought was heathenish and barbaric. But many clergymen became scholars, diligently recording the history, languages, and folklore of the Aztecs and other pre-conquest civilizations. In addition, some clergymen became famous as champions and protectors of the Indians. One of the first and best-known of these was a Dominican friar named Bartolomé de Las Casas. In 1552 he published *A Brief Relation of the Destruction of the Indies,* a grim account of the devastation wrought by the conquistadores in the years immediately following the Spanish invasion, when the whites killed a great many Indians by forcing them to labor in the gold and silver mines without food or rest. Las Casas was an early leader of the fight for laws to protect Indian rights and freedoms; he helped bring about the abolishment of the encomiendas. And although the church in Mexico did shelter some greedy, intolerant, or lazy clergymen, there were always those who, like Las Casas, sincerely tried to improve the lives of the oppressed and downtrodden. Even the most tolerant and well-meaning churchmen, however, viewed Mexico's Native American people as childlike beings who needed to be helped and guided to Western ways. No European of the colonial era would have recognized the Indians as equals or felt that they should remain in control of their country and way of life.

The European powers of the time believed unswervingly that they had a right—even a duty—to claim colonies in Africa, Asia, and the Americas. One reason for establishing colonies was to add to the parent country's prestige; another was to "save" the native peoples by turning them into Christians. But the principal reason behind the drive to colonize was money. Spain regarded its colonies as economic ventures, sources of income for the parent country. The main goal of colonial policies and administrators was to extract as much wealth as possible from the colonies and ship it back to Spain.

New Spain was Spain's richest and most productive colony. At first its conquerors concentrated on gold and silver. Each year enormous amounts of these precious metals were sent to Spain in armadas called treasure fleets. Eventually, though, the output of the mines diminished somewhat (although Mexico is still one of the world's major producers of silver), and other products gained importance. These included cochineal, a red dye made from ants, and indigo, a blue plant dye. Sugar, cacao (from which chocolate is made), cotton, tobacco, rope, and vanilla were also exported to Spain.

The colony played a dual role in Spain's economic plan. Not only was it a source of raw materials to be used by the parent country, but it was also a market for manufactured goods made by Spanish workers. Woven fabrics, clothing and shoes, wine, candles, paper, and steel and iron tools were among the products that were shipped from Spain to Mexico. The parent country was enriched by two sets of taxes paid by ship captains and merchants: on raw materials leaving the colony *and* on manufactured goods entering it. To ensure a market for Spanish goods, the colonists were forbidden to trade with other countries or colonies and discouraged from setting up factories and industries of their own. The result was that colonies such as New Spain were drained of their resources but got little back from Spain in the way of investment or development. In time some of the people of New Spain came to resent the high taxes they paid to Spain and the way the colony was exploited for Spain's benefit. This resentment was strongest among the people known as *criollos.*

The criollos, or creoles, were white people of Spanish descent who had been born in Mexico—in other words, colonists of the second generation or later. The *peninsulares,* on the other hand, were people who had come to Mexico directly from Spain (which is a peninsula). The peninsulares were usually called *gachupines* by the criollos; the term was a mild insult, but its meaning is lost.

Together the peninsulares and the criollos made up the white or European population of New Spain, and in this respect they were united against the rest of the population. Alexander von Humboldt, a German scientist who visited Mexico in the early years of the 19th century, explained in his 1811 book, *A Political Essay on the Kingdom of New Spain,* "In America, the skin, more or less white, is what dictates the class that an individual occupies in society. A white, even if he rides barefoot on horseback, considers himself a member of the nobility of the country." The poorest and least educated white person felt and acted superior to Indians, mestizos, and blacks of all ranks and conditions.

Within the white population, however, a sharp class distinction separated the peninsulares from the criollos. Although by 1810 criollos outnumbered peninsulares more than 30 to 1, the peninsulares held all the highest positions in the colonial administration, the army, and the church, and the criollos were generally confined to lower-ranking positions. The criollos dominated only in the town councils, and these councils had little real power. The peninsulares regarded the criollos as ignorant provincial bumpkins, while the criollos regarded the gachupines as arrogant snobs. A more profound difference lay in their attitudes toward Spain. The peninsulares were time-serving officials who considered Spain their home. Most of the criollos, on the other hand, had no practical connection with Spain, although they retained feelings of loyalty to the crown and the church and, when they could afford it, sent their children to Europe to be educated. Unlike the gachupines, who could not wait to get back to Spain, the criollos devoted themselves to amassing property, wealth, and status in Mexico. They therefore grew impatient with the way the peninsulares monopolized the colony's top positions, and they chafed at Spain's tight control of the Mexican economy.

Many criollos in New Spain and in other Spanish colonies throughout Central and South America were coming to view Spanish rule as at odds with their own interests. Simón Bolívar, a Venezuelan criollo who helped liberate much of South America from Spanish rule in the early years of the 19th century, described the criollos' resentment in a letter written in 1815:

We have been molested by a system which has not only deprived us of our rights but has kept us in a state of perpetual childhood with regard to public affairs. . . . So negative was our state that I can find nothing comparable in any other civilized society, examine as I may the history of all ages and the politics of all nations. Is it not an outrage and a violation of human rights to expect a land so happily endowed, so vast, rich, and populous, to remain merely passive?

Ironically, the resentment felt by Bolívar and other criollos echoed the despair felt by the masses of landless, hopeless peasants—for whom the criollos felt little sympathy.

In the second half of the 18th century, the fires of criollo discontent were fanned by happenings elsewhere in the world. In Spain, the Hapsburg dynasty, or royal family, was replaced by the Bourbon dynasty, and the Bourbon kings launched a series of economic and administrative reforms in New Spain. These reforms streamlined the colony's bureaucracy and opened up free trade between Mexico and other nations, but at the same time they brought new gachupin officials to the colony to prosper at the expense of the criollos. The Bourbons succeeded in boosting the colony's economy, but the benefits went to Spain and the peninsulares, further angering the criollos. And when the Bourbons, fearful that the church and the pope were becoming too powerful in the Spanish colonies, exiled the Jesuit religious order from the Americas in 1767, Mexico's criollos, mestizos, and Indians alike were outraged.

The American Revolution of 1776–83 affected both Spain and Mexico. Spain was alarmed to see a major colonial power lose control of one of its colonies, and in Mexico a handful of progressive thinkers secretly passed bootleg copies of Thomas Jefferson's Declaration of Independence from hand to hand and eagerly discussed the idea of liberty for Mexico. These visionaries were few in number, however. The great majority of criollos, even those who were fed up with pushy peninsulares and high taxes, remained loyal to the Spanish crown. They wanted change, but not radical, extreme change; their motto was "Long live the king, and to hell with bad government." Thus years before Mexico gained its independence, a rift existed in the ranks of the criollos between the liberals and the conservatives.

The liberals had progressive notions and wanted to make sweeping changes in society and government. Some of them were radicals, who favored extreme changes such as revolution and democracy. Others were more moderate, hoping for peaceful progress; they wanted to introduce reforms but not necessarily to overthrow the existing order completely. Liberal ideas tended to win support from the lower urban classes and the rural peasants, because these groups had the most to gain by change and reform.

The conservatives regarded the idea of change with caution, or even alarm. They wanted to preserve the existing order more or less intact. Some of them were reactionaries, or extremists, who refused to consider any changes at all—they felt that the way things had been done for 300 years was good enough for them. But other conservatives were more moderate. They were willing to accept the idea of limited change, but they wanted the process to be slow and controlled. For example, nearly all the criollos wanted to wrest control of the administration from the peninsulares, but most them were nevertheless conservative in their thinking, for they expected that Mexico would still be part of the Spanish empire and that the class structure of society would not change. Conservative ideas tended to appeal to high-ranking military and church officials, to aristocrats, and to wealthy landowners, for these had the most to lose by change. They had enjoyed a privileged way of life for many years and did not want to lose their privileges. Although liberals and conservatives agreed on some points, most of the time they were at odds. This opposition between liberals and conservatives was to become the driving force in Mexican politics.

The rift between liberals and conservatives grew wider when the Spanish American colonies received word that a bloody revolution in

France had brought an end to the French monarchy. Like the American Revolution, the French Revolution of 1789 was an expression of the wave of rational, progressive thinking that arose in the 18th century. During this period, now referred to as the Enlightenment, social philosophers encouraged people to reexamine their ideas about such matters as the privileges and duties of kings and the proper relationship between the individual and the state. After seeing Louis XVI of France beheaded on the guillotine, other monarchs naturally enough tried to keep their subjects from thinking along progressive lines, and Enlightenment writings such as Thomas Paine's *The Rights of Man* and Jean-Jacques Rousseau's *The Social Contract* were officially banned in the Spanish colonies. But some educated, liberal criollos got hold of smuggled copies of these books.

Another widely circulated liberal document was *Letter to the Spanish-Americans,* published in 1799 by Juan Pablo Viscardo y Guzman, a Jesuit who had been banished from Peru. He declared, "Nature has separated us from Spain by immense seas. A son who found himself at such a distance from his father would doubtless be a fool if, in the management of his own affairs, he constantly awaited the decision of his father." People who read Viscardo's pamphlet and other Enlightenment works began to think about changing New Spain's relationship with the parent country to give the criollos a greater say in government.

At the same time, a new sentiment was growing throughout Spanish America. It was *patría,* or nationalism. Separated by wide seas from Spain, grown distant from the parent country by generations of colonial life, and tired of being treated as second-class Spaniards, the criollos began to think of themselves as a new, distinct people: the Americans. Wrote Humboldt in *A Political Essay on the Kingdom of New Spain,* "The natives [meaning criollos] prefer the denomination of *Americans* to that of Creoles. Since the peace of Versailles, and, in particular, since the year 1789, we frequently hear proudly declared: 'I am not a *Spaniard,* I am an *American!*', words that betray the workings of a long resentment."

Some of these newly proud Americans regarded themselves as specifically Mexican, and a spirit of *mexicanismo,* an enthusiasm for all things Mexican, became fashionable in New Spain. Filled with a burgeoning sense of Mexican identity, some criollos began flaunting their regional accents and other differences from the gachupines, rather than trying to hide these characteristics. Members of the criollo upper class also took a new interest in the splendid architecture and arts of the remaining Aztec ruins. Few of these criollo aristocrats, however, took any interest in the descendants of the Aztecs, the contemporary Indians and mestizos. Even the most ardently liberal criollos were seldom troubled by the dismal status of the lower classes.

The criollos were used to thinking of society as an enormous pyramid. At the top, a handful of Spanish bureaucrats held most of the power. Below them, but still near the top, were the aristocratic and wealthy criollos, and below them was the growing criollo middle class of shopowners, tradespeople, and workers. Then came the most successful and prosperous mestizos. At the bottom of the pyramid, nearly crushed by the oppressive weight of those above, were the peasant masses, mostly laborers, with a few independent farmers in remote districts. The peasant class included not only most people of mixed blood but also the single largest group in Mexico's population, its Native Americans. Most of the criollos who wanted to change things merely hoped to rearrange the top layers of the pyramid; they expected that the bottom layer would remain as it had always been.

Following centuries of Spanish domination and gachupin arrogance, the Bourbon reforms and the expulsion of the Jesuits, and the American and French revolutions, the 19th century dawned on a Mexico that was simmering with discontent and frustration. Before long that frustration erupted into open rebellion.

CHAPTER ONE NOTES

p. 11   "In America, . . ." Alexander von Humboldt, *Political Essay on the Kingdom of New Spain*; quoted in Michael Meyer and William Sherman, *The Course of Mexican History* (New York: Oxford, 1991), pp. 276–277.

p. 12   "We have been molested . . ." Simón Bolívar, "Cartas del Libertador," in *The Origins of the Latin American Revolutions, 1808–1826*, ed. R.A. Humphreys and John Lynch (New York: Knopf, 1966), p. 263.

p. 14 "Nature has separated us from Spain . . ." Pablo Viscardo y Guzman, "Lettre aux Espagnols-Americans, Par un de Leur Compatriots," in William Spence Robertson, *Rise of the Spanish-American Republics As Told in the Lives of Their Liberators* (New York: Collier, 1961), p. 39 (originally published by Appleton, 1918).

p. 14 "The natives prefer the domination . . ." von Humboldt, *Political Essay on the Kingdom of New Spain,* trans. and ed. John Black (London, 1811) vol. I, p. 205.

FATHER HIDALGO'S REVOLT

The colonial era in Mexico is sometimes portrayed as a long, drowsy "siesta" in which history bypassed Spanish America and nothing much happened for 300 years. This image is false. Although the structure of New Spain's society and the nature of its government and economy changed little over the centuries, many noteworthy artistic achievements took place, and life in the colony was also disrupted by cataclysmic events such as famines, plagues, and earthquakes. In addition there were political upheavals—nearly 100 conspiracies and rebellions against Spain between 1521 and 1810. Most of these were small local affairs that posed no real threat to Spanish rule, but a few of the Indian insurgencies, or uprisings, were larger and more serious. All the revolts before 1810, however, were isolated bonfires rather than sweeping infernos. Spanish officials and armed forces put down each revolt before it could attract widespread support. But a rebellion that flared up in 1810 ended by igniting all of Mexico.

The rebellion was brought about by events in Spain. King Charles IV of the Bourbon dynasty came to the Spanish throne in 1788 and proved a weak and ineffective ruler. He named Manuel de Godoy, his wife's lover, as prime minister of Spain, and Godoy's misguided policies led Spain into war with France. In 1808 French troops led by Napoleon Bonaparte invaded Spain and took the king prisoner. Charles gave up the kingship in favor of his son Ferdinand, but Napoleon refused to allow Ferdinand to take the throne. Instead he named his brother, Joseph Bonaparte, the new king of Spain. Many parts of Spain raised troops to resist Bonaparte rule, and the French army dug in for a long siege.

Across the Atlantic Ocean, the colonies of Spanish America were appalled by events in the parent country. New Spain was thrown into confusion. No one wanted the colony to fall into French hands, but the various groups within Mexico could not agree on who was officially in charge now that the rightful king had been deposed. A few radicals, or extreme liberals, claimed that the time had come for independence. But at the other extreme, royalist peninsulares insisted that the viceroy must continue to govern the colony in King Ferdinand's name. Many of the criollos, especially in provincial regions outside the capital, fell somewhere in between. While they remained loyal to Ferdinand, they wanted to form juntas, or temporary local governments, to manage their own affairs until Ferdinand regained his throne. Some of them hoped that even after the Spanish king was back on his throne these local governments would manage to keep some of their authority.

One event during this period of turmoil had long-lasting effects. To the alarm of the royalist peninsulares, Viceroy José de Iturrigaray began to side with the criollos. Iturrigaray believed that the resistance forces back in Spain had no chance of holding out against the French army. And if Spain fell to France, he thought, New Spain would certainly become independent. But Iturrigaray had no intention of letting himself be swept aside if the colony gained independence—he wanted to be the first king of the new Mexican nation. The peninsulares, who remained fiercely loyal to the Spanish throne, realized that Iturrigaray would not try to control the restless criollos. Indeed, he might actually hand the colony over to them. So they took matters into their own hands.

On the night of September 15, 1808, a small band of armed pen-insulares carried out a *coup d'état* (a French phrase, meaning "blow against the state," that refers to the overthrow of a government by forces from within). The peninsulares sneaked into the viceregal palace and arrested the viceroy. He was unceremoniously shipped off to prison in Spain, and the next several viceroys were chosen by the peninsulares.

At first glance, the coup against Iturrigaray seems like a small incident in the panorama of Mexican history. Only one man—a palace guard—was killed, and the rule of the peninsulares was unbroken. Yet as historian Lesley Byrd Simpson points out in his book *Many Mexicos*, the event set a pattern that was to be repeated many times. When they ousted the legally appointed viceroy, the conservative peninsulares opened the door for other groups to use force to impose their own ideas upon the state. They fostered the notion that anyone who could muster enough guns or followers had the right to take control of Mexico. In later periods the coup d'état was viewed by some as an acceptable tool of statecraft, and at times government by military force became almost a way of life.

Following Napoleon's invasion of Spain, the political confusion in New Spain was made worse by economic stress from two sources. First, trade between the colony and the parent country was interrupted, causing shortages of many imported goods. Then a severe drought led to shortages of corn, bringing high food prices and fears of famine. All these factors created tension and instability in Mexico. Revolutionaries and conspirators took advantage of the troubled spirit of the times to form plots against the colonial government. These conspiracies were often disguised as social or literary clubs. Most were the work of liberal criollos, but some involved Native Americans and mestizos as well. The royalist government used spies and paid informants to investigate all suspicious groups and meetings, hoping to ferret out the ringleaders before they could launch revolts. In the fall of 1810, the authorities in Mexico City heard of a conspiracy in Querétaro, a town north of the capital. The head of the conspiracy was said to be a 57-year-old priest named Miguel Hidalgo y Costilla, who lived not far away in the small village of Dolores.

Hidalgo had been in trouble with the authorities before. The son of a middle-class provincial criollo, he entered the priesthood in 1778. At first his future seemed bright. In 1784 he won a prize for essays he had written about religion, and the university official who awarded the prize wrote to Hidalgo, "With the greatest joy in my heart, I foresee that you will become a light placed in a candlestick, or a city upon a hill." The pious scholar would no doubt have been astonished if he had foreseen just what kind of inspiration Hidalgo was destined to provide.

Hidalgo's problems with the church and the colonial government began in the 1790s. He was accused of contradicting the holy teachings—for example, by saying that hell did not exist and that sex out of wedlock was not a sin (in fact, Hidalgo had a mistress and several illegitimate daughters). He was also rumored to speak of more treacherous matters: revolution and independence. Nothing was proved against him, however, and he was permitted to resume his post in Dolores, in what is today the state of Guanajuato. There he spent more time helping the local peasants develop new industries—such as beekeeping and silk-making—than he did preaching and listening to confessions.

By 1810 Hidalgo had become involved in a conspiracy to overthrow Spanish rule in Mexico. His motives were complex. Undoubtedly he felt resentment against the Spanish-born peninsulares who rose to positions of power and influence while provincial criollos like himself were condemned to obscurity. Yet more than simple resentment lay behind his actions. In the tradition of liberal, compassionate clergymen that stretched back to Bartolomé de Las Casas, Hidalgo hoped to improve the lot of the oppressed masses. Unlike the great majority of criollos, he had a genuine sympathy for the Indians, whom he planned to enlist in a revolutionary army. Hidalgo wanted to end the domination of Spain and the peninsulares, but he also wanted to bring about a new social order, one in which the country's poor people would have some freedoms and a greater share of the land and its wealth.

Among the other members of the conspiracy were two army officers named Ignacio Allende, who probably introduced Hidalgo to the group in the first place, and Juan Aldama. Along with Hidalgo, they became the chief plotters. They planned to launch their revolt in December, but the authorities got wind of their plans and moved against them in September, arresting several minor conspirators. Allende, Aldama, and Hidalgo escaped arrest and met in Hidalgo's church in Dolores. They knew that they risked execution as traitors if they surrendered, so they decided to go ahead with the rebellion. On September 16 Hidalgo rang the church bells to summon the Indian workers from the surrounding fields and workshops; he also freed everyone in the village jail, and the released prisoners gratefully joined the group at the church. Hidalgo addressed this little crowd with fiery words.

Many versions of Hidalgo's speech exist, but all are merely guesses, for his exact words were not recorded. It is known, however, that he urged his hearers to demand liberty and the return of lands unjustly seized from them by the Spanish. He called on the Blessed Virgin of Guadalupe to aid the rebel cause. This was a powerful appeal, for the Lady of Guadalupe—a vision of the Virgin Mary seen by an Indian in 1531—was the special patroness of the Native American Christians. Hidalgo rallied the crowd with a cry of "Long live Liberty! Long live the Virgin of Guadalupe!" and the crowd roared back, "Death to the gachupines!" This cry, the *Grito de Dolores* (shout of Dolores), is regarded by modern Mexicans as the true beginning of their country's independence.

With Hidalgo at their head and a banner of the Virgin of Guadalupe waving above, the rebels moved toward the town of San Miguel. The revolutionary army grew as it marched. Thousands of farm laborers and mine workers, brandishing their tools as weapons, joined Hidalgo. The rebels captured San Miguel without much trouble because the local militia joined the uprising. The same thing happened at the town of Celaya. But after each victory the triumphant army turned into an angry mob, raging through the streets to kill the Europeans and loot their homes and shops.

Hidalgo has been criticized for his followers' violence and lack of discipline, but in truth there was little he could do about it. Like many revolutionaries before him and after, he found that he had unleashed a force that he could not easily control. The rebel army consisted almost entirely of Indian peasants (and some mestizos). They were eager to turn the tables against their hated white overlords after centuries of oppression, and they could not resist the temptation to revenge themselves on their enemies by whatever means came to hand. Hidalgo and his criollo followers had believed that the army would attack the peninsulares and leave the criollos alone, but they soon saw that they were wrong. In every community through which it passed, the rebel army turned its fury against the entire white population. Hidalgo, who had no military training and no experience in controlling large numbers of men, refused to turn command of the army over to Allende or one of the other military men—and even a trained officer would probably have found it hard to dampen the passions of the unruly mob.

Hidalgo accepted the killing and looting as a necessary evil. His was a revolutionary movement, and he believed that the old order had to be destroyed before the new one could begin. But the goals of the revolt and the shape of that new order were never spelled out in great detail. Forced to act before their plans had been completed and then rushed along on the swift tide of events, Hidalgo and the other leaders of the insurgency never put together a formal plan for governing the country. It is clear from some of Hidalgo's statements that he wanted Mexico to become an independent nation, governed by Mexicans instead of by Spaniards. He seems to have planned some sort of representative assembly to write a constitution and make laws, although he also insisted that Mexico would remain part of the Spanish empire, loyal to King Ferdinand and the Roman Catholic church. One important step toward establishing Mexican independence would be to win official recognition from other nations. Hidalgo thought that the United States, which had recently gained its own independence, would readily grant such recognition to the Mexican insurgents. Twice he sent messengers to request U.S. recognition, but both men were seized by the royalist authorities before they got out of Mexico.

Some of the decrees that Hidalgo issued as commander of the revolutionary forces hint at the reforms he hoped to make in the new Mexico. One decree said that all lands inhabited by the Indians would be worked by the Indians alone, for their own profit. Hidalgo talked of breaking up the great estates and latifundia of the wealthy aristocrats and giving the land to the poor. Another decree called for all African and mulatto slaves to be set free; Hidalgo was the first of the Spanish-American liberators to attack slavery.

On September 28 the rebel force arrived at Guanajuato, a provincial capital. Hidalgo promised to spare the lives of the royalists in the city if they surrendered. But the Spanish commandant had heard of the massacres in San Miguel and Celaya, and he did not believe Hidalgo. So he gathered the city's treasury and its royalist citizens into the Alhóndiga, a large building used to store grain, hoping to hold off the rebels until the viceroy sent help.

At first the royalists had the upper hand. From the high walls of the Alhóndiga they poured bullets into the poorly armed army below, killing hundreds of insurgents. But the Alhóndiga had a weak spot: its wooden door. The rebels used torches to burn down the door and then rushed into the makeshift fortress, killing most of those inside. Lucas Alamán, a resident of Guanajuato, was 18 years old at the time. He witnessed the attack on the Alhóndiga and survived its gory aftermath. Later he became a well-known conservative historian. In his five-volume history of Mexico, published from 1849 to 1852, he recalled the events of Guanajuato:

> When the insurgents had taken the Alhóndiga they gave rein to their vengeance. In vain those who had surrendered begged on their knees for mercy. . . . The building presented a most horrible spectacle. The food that had been stored there was strewn about everywhere; naked bodies lay half-buried in maize [corn], or in money, and everything was spotted with blood.

More than 500 royalists and more than 2,000 rebels—mostly Indians—died in the battle of Guanajuato.

Allende, Hidalgo, and the other members of the original conspiracy had hoped that criollos throughout the land would rise up and join them once they declared war on the Spanish. At first the rebels' success did inspire similar uprisings among discontented criollos as well as among the peasants. But after Guanajuato, Hidalgo received almost no support from the criollos, probably because of the violent, uncontrolled nature of the uprising. The criollos despised the peninsulares—but they were terrified of Hidalgo's mob. The revolt had taken on some of the qualities of a race and class war. Because most criollos could not bring themselves to side with the nonwhite rebels, whom they deeply feared and distrusted, they were forced to side with the Spanish authorities.

The authorities acted quickly against the insurgents. The viceroy proclaimed them traitors and offered a handsome reward for Allende, Hidalgo, and Aldama, dead or alive. A high-ranking bishop denounced Hidalgo as a renegade priest and a disturber of the peace. Governors, mayors, town councillors, and other worried officials throughout Mexico hastened to put statements in the newspapers, announcing their loyalty to Spain and their opposition to Hidalgo. Then the viceroy sent 13,000 royalist troops into the field against the rebels. A few of the soldiers were Spanish, but most were criollo and mestizo militiamen who remained loyal to the viceroy; the officers were Spaniards and high-ranking criollos. The two royalist generals, Torcuato Trujillo and Félix Calleja, had orders to destroy Hidalgo and his ragtag army.

For a time Hidalgo seemed unstoppable. He marched on Valladolid, west of Mexico City, and the town promptly surrendered. Other towns followed. Within a month Hidalgo controlled much of central Mexico west of the capital. He and his followers exulted that a new era was dawning in Mexico. All that remained was to seize the capital. Hidalgo led his army of about 80,000 toward Mexico City.

The rebels met General Trujillo's 7,000-man force at a place called Monte de las Cruces, just west of the capital. Although overwhelmingly outnumbered, the royalists gave a good account of themselves. They were forced to retreat, but they inflicted heavy losses on the insurgents before they fled, leaving Hidalgo in possession of the hills overlooking Mexico City.

This was a crucial point in Hidalgo's revolt. Allende and some of his other supporters urged him to follow up his victory over Trujillo with a quick strike at Mexico City. But Hidalgo turned away from the capital, perhaps because he felt he had lost too many men and too much ammunition to make a winning attack, or perhaps because he feared the damage his mob might do if turned loose in the capital. Whatever the reason, he ordered a march northwest to Guadalajara.

Some military historians think that if Hidalgo had attacked Mexico City he would have been victorious, and his revolt would have ended in triumph after just a few weeks of fighting. Others, however, claim that he was wise to retreat, and that even if he had been able to take the capital, the city would have been virtually destroyed and impossible to govern. At any rate, the retreat from Mexico City had a disturbing result. Many of the insurgents, disappointed that they were not to march on the capital, lost interest in the revolt and drifted back to their homes and farms. After a sharp skirmish with General Calleja's army, the rebel desertions increased. By the time the insurgents had occupied Guadalajara, their army had shrunk considerably. Allende at once began recruiting and training new soldiers, and before long he had brought the rebel army back up to 80,000.

Enthusiasm for the revolt was still strong in many regions south and west of Mexico City, but the tide began to turn against Hidalgo when General Calleja recaptured Guanajuato. Then, with 6,000 well-trained and well-armed men, Calleja marched on Guadalajara. His army and Hidalgo's collided on January 17, 1811, at a place called Calderón. The general was a brilliant field commander; his troops soon threw the rebel force into disarray. The insurgents vastly outnumbered Calleja's men, yet they failed to rout the royalists in six hours of fighting. Then a grass fire swept across the battlefield, probably started by an explosion in an ammunition wagon. This accident broke the nerve of the rebels, and most of them fled. Hidalgo and Allende managed to avoid capture. With 1,000 or so followers they headed north, hoping to gather new strength in Texas, which was part of Mexico but had few Spanish officials.

Their hopes faded as they pressed northward across the barren desert. No new recruits joined them. Some followers left their ranks. One of the deserters, Ignacio Elizondo, joined a troop of royalists and set up an ambush along Hidalgo's line of march. On February 21, near the town of Monclova in present-day Coahuila state, Hidalgo and the other insurgents were surrounded and taken prisoner. The lesser leaders of the revolt were executed on the spot, but Hidalgo and Allende were shipped to the city of Chihuahua for trial. Allende received a quick traitor's execution—he was shot through the back. Hidalgo's trial took longer. As a priest, he had to be examined by the Inquisition, the enforcing arm of Spanish Catholicism, before he was turned over to the firing squad on July 30. In revenge for the slaying of the Spanish in the Alhóndiga at Guanajuato, the authorities displayed the heads of Hidalgo, Allende, and Aldama on the walls of the Alhóndiga for 10 years—a grisly reminder of the revolutionaries' fate, and a warning to anyone else who might dream of opposing the government.

Father Hidalgo was a remarkable man. Certainly he was neither the perfect saint of liberal legends nor the bloody-handed butcher that the royalists made him out to be. He possessed the ability to rouse the masses, but not always the skill to lead them well. He cried out for

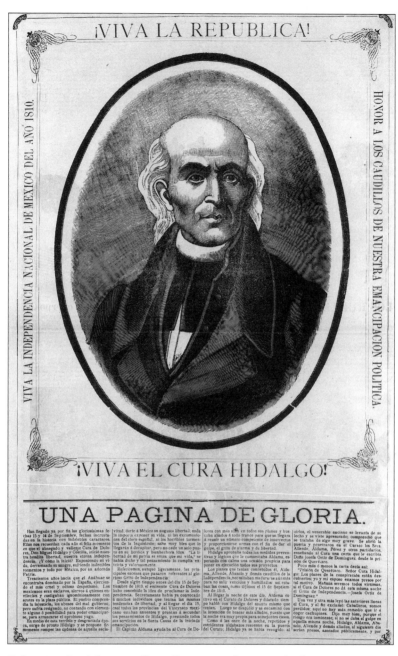

Father Miguel Hidalgo y Costilla, a village priest, who in 1810 fired a peasant army into revolt against Spanish rule. The royalist authorities executed Hidalgo as a traitor, but today he is honored as one of Mexico's greatest patriots. (Library of Congress)

reform and justice, but plunged the country into a bitter war. Above all, Hidalgo was a visionary. He envisioned a Mexico without the injustices of colonialism, and he fired others with that vision. Perhaps most important, Hidalgo was the first of the Spanish-American liberators to care deeply about the needs of the land-hungry and oppressed Native Americans. He promised them not just a package of vague and abstract rights but something real that they desperately wanted: land of their own. They did not forget that promise. A hundred years after Hidalgo's time, land reform was to be a key issue in the political and social movements of 20th-century Mexico.

Today Hidalgo is revered as the Mexican George Washington, the father of his country's liberty. September 16, the anniversary of the Grito de Dolores, is Mexico's independence day, and the church bell that Hidalgo rang that day now hangs in an honored position in Mexico City.

CHAPTER TWO NOTES

pp. 19–20   "With the greatest joy . . ." William Spence Robertson, *Rise of the Spanish-American Republics as Told in the Lives of Their Liberators* (New York: Collier, 1961), p. 85.

p. 23   "When the insurgents . . ." Lucas Alamán, *Historía de México* (originally published 1842) in Lesley Byrd Simpson, *Many Mexicos* (Berkeley, Calif.: Univ. of California Press, 1966), p. 213.

REBELS AGAINST ROYALISTS

The revolt against the royalists lost strength after the rebels' defeat at Calderón, but it did not die altogether with Hidalgo. In many parts of Mexico, especially in the south and west, bands of insurgents continued to elude the Spanish troops and to call for revolution. After Hidalgo's death another priest, Mexico's second great hero of independence, stepped forward to lead the fight.

José María Morelos y Pavón came from a background more humble than Hidalgo's. He was a poor mestizo from Valladolid in western Mexico. As a young man he worked as a mule driver, leading pack caravans along the mountain trails. When he was 25 years old or so, he began studying at the university in Valladolid; he became a priest a few years later, in 1797. Like Hidalgo, Morelos was deeply dissatisfied with the state of affairs in Mexico. When Hidalgo launched the revolt in 1810, Morelos hastened to join the insurgents. He was assigned by Hidalgo to carry the revolution into southern Mexico and there, amid the inhospitable jungle-covered mountains, he recruited a small but capable rebel force. Although some Native Americans rallied to him as they had rallied to Hidalgo, Morelos was much more successful in attracting mestizos—and even a few criollos—to the revolutionary cause than Hidalgo had been.

Morelos's style of fighting, too, was very different from Hidalgo's. Instead of pitched battles with a large, unwieldy army, Morelos favored guerrilla warfare. After surprise attacks on royalist militia posts and supply trains, Morelos and his guerrilleros would stealthily disappear back into the countryside. This tactic worked well, and Morelos and his followers broke the royalist hold on much of southern and western Mexico. After the executions of Allende and Hidalgo in 1811, Morelos kept up his guerrilla warfare against the royalists. He was aided by a handful of other rebel leaders who were active in the region along Mexico's southwestern coast. These included Vicente Guerrero, Manuel Félix Fernández (who adopted the name Guadalupe Victoria in honor of victory for the followers of the Virgin of Guadalupe), and Father Mariano Matamoros, a priest who was one of Morelos's best battle commanders.

For four turbulent years, Morelos's insurgents battled the royalist army of General Calleja in a deadly game of tag through the highlands and valleys of Mexico. Calleja came close to winning in 1812, when he trapped the rebels in the town of Cuautla, not far south of the capital. During a 72-day siege, Morelos and his men endured frightful suffering; many died of starvation. Finally, in desperation, the rebels crept out of Cuautla in utter silence one night. When Calleja realized what was happening he attacked, but a large part of the rebel army escaped. In November of that year Morelos achieved one of his biggest successes when he captured Oaxaca, a large and important city in southern Mexico. In 1813 he took the western port of Acapulco after a long siege. But he was never able to move against Mexico City—the capital was well-protected by royalist troops.

Morelos was more than a military leader. He was a statesman who gave much thought to the future of his country. He wanted Mexico to be independent, and he wanted it to be governed by civilians guided by a constitution, not by generals who ruled at gunpoint. In the fall of 1813 he organized a meeting of leading insurgents in the town of Chilpancingo. The congress of Chilpancingo marked two milestones in the wars for independence. It formally declared Mexico an independent nation, free of all ties with Spain, and it produced a set of principles to serve as the basis for a national constitution.

José María Morelos y Pavón took over leadership of the revolt after Hidalgo's death. In this portrait by 20th-century Mexican artist Diego Rivera, Morelos wields the sword of battle in one hand; the other holds Mexico's first constitution. (Library of Congress)

These principles outlined the kind of government that the revolutionaries hoped to set up. Like the United States government, it was to be divided into three branches, the legislative, the executive, and the judicial. Male citizens would elect legislative representatives (even radical revolutionaries did not go so far as to consider votes for women in the early 19th century), and these representatives in turn would appoint the president and the judges. Slavery would be outlawed. People would not be divided into classes by skin color, race, or place of origin—the old labels would be discarded, and all people would be called simply "Americans." The same laws would apply to rich and poor alike, without exception. Roman Catholicism would be the official religion of Mexico; the practice of any other religion would be against the law.

The congress of Chilpancingo had to break up hurriedly when royalist soldiers advanced on the town. But in late 1814 the congress met again at Apatzingán, another town in the southwestern mountains, to write Mexico's first constitution. On paper—at least as far as the revolutionaries were concerned—Mexico was now a liberated country with a formal government. But the rebels had no printing presses and were unable to communicate their constitution across the land, as they had hoped. In fact, the constitution was most widely circulated by the royalist newspapers, which printed it only to denounce it. Both the Chilpancingo declaration of independence and the Apatzingán constitution were symbols of hope rather than political realities—the insurgents could not enforce them. Most of the viceroyalty of New Spain remained firmly in royalist hands.

By this time the fortunes of war were turning against Morelos. General Calleja had been made viceroy of New Spain and was determined to end the insurgency. The royalists had recaptured Oaxaca and other rebel strongholds, the ranks of the insurgents were dwindling, and the revolution was on the run. At Valladolid Morelos's forces suffered a stinging defeat by the royalists; during this battle a criollo colonel named Agustín de Iturbide captured Mariano Matamoros and had him executed. After Valladolid many of the insurgents lost faith in Morelos's leadership, and the revolution split into quarreling factions.

Throughout most of 1815 the rebels managed to stay one step ahead of the royalists. In the fall they decided to move their headquarters from the southwest to a region called Puebla in the southeast, where there were fewer royalist troops on the prowl. To reach Puebla, however, they would have to pass through a stretch of royalist territory. There, on November 5, they encountered a detachment of 600 royalist troops. Morelos, who was guarding the rebel convoy, fought off the

AN ANCIENT AND MODERN CAPITAL

Mexico City is a city of extremes. It is the oldest metropolis in the Americas and the largest urban center in the world. It is a city of great beauty, and also a city with great problems.

Before the Spanish came, Mexico City was called Tenochtitlán. Founded in the early 14th century, it was the capital of the Aztec state, built upon an island in the center of a large lake called Texcoco. Tenochtitlán held many huge stone palaces and temples; canals ran through the city instead of streets, and long causeways connected the city to the mainland. But after the Spanish conquered the Aztecs they destroyed Tenochtitlán. Bernal Díaz del Castillo, one of Cortés's soldiers, later wrote of the fallen capital, "I thought that no land like it would ever be discovered in the whole world. But today all that I then saw is overthrown and destroyed; nothing is left standing."

The Spanish filled in the lake and built their own capital, Ciudád de México, or Mexico City, on the ruins of Tenochtitlán, using stones from the Aztec structures. The surviving Aztecs were banished to districts on the fringe of the city, which later became the ever-growing Indian quarters of the new capital. The center of Tenochtitlán had been a large open area called the Zócalo, ringed with temples and palaces; today the Zócalo, also called the Plaza of the Constitution, is still the center of downtown Mexico City, with the national palace on one side and the largest Roman Catholic cathedral in Spanish America on another.

Many vestiges of Mexico City's ancient past can be seen in the modern city. Over the centuries, workers digging ditches or laying the foundations of buildings have uncovered Aztec relics—statues of jade, huge disk-shaped stones carved with royalists long enough to allow the members of the congress to escape, but in the end he was captured and marched to Mexico City in chains.

News of his capture caused intense interest in the capital, where crowds lined the streets to see him pass. The authorities were afraid that pro-revolutionary mobs might riot if Morelos were executed in

elaborate symbols, and hand-hewn building blocks—in the heart of the capital. In the late 1970s the remains of the Great Temple of the Aztecs were unearthed near the cathedral. These ruins were carefully excavated, and now they stand next to the cathedral that replaced them. Symbols of the different eras in Mexican history can also be seen in the Plaza of Three Cultures, which has Aztec ruins, Spanish colonial buildings, and modern Mexican architecture.

Mexico City today faces problems as grave as any it has seen in its long history. The city's population increases by about 2,000 people a day, partly because of a high birth rate and partly because many rural Mexicans migrate to the capital in search of jobs or a more sophisticated life. In 1880 Mexico City had 200,000 inhabitants. Fifty years later it just had passed the 1 million mark. Fifty years after that, in 1980, its population was 15 million. In 1990 it had passed 21 million, and demographers—scientists who study population trends—predict a population of more than 31 million by the year 2000. This huge and growing population places tremendous pressure on the city. There is a shortage of adequate housing; downtown Mexico City is ringed by vast tracts of slums and squatters' shacks. Unemployment is high. Water shortages are becoming increasingly common, and a brown haze hangs over the city—the air pollution from some 3 million vehicles is among the worst in the world.

To the Aztecs, Tenochtitlán was a garden in the midst of barrenness, a city "precious as jade." Modern Mexico City also boasts splendid artworks, gracious boulevards, and lush gardens. But Mexico's urban planners warn that the beauty of the capital can be preserved only if the poverty that blights it is eliminated.

Mexico City, so after his trial he was taken to a village north of the capital and shot. But the map of modern Mexico shows how this high-minded freedom fighter was later honored. There is a state named Morelos just south of Mexico City, and Valladolid—the city where Morelos was born and where he suffered his worst defeat in battle—was renamed Morelia in 1828 and bears that name today.

The insurrection had lasted for five years, but its two principal leaders were now dead, and much of the territory that had been won by the rebels had been reclaimed by the royalists. A few rebel leaders did remain active in remote districts. The most important of these were Vicente Guerrero, who had about 1,000 troops in the Oaxaca region, and Guadalupe Victoria, who had about 2,000 in Puebla and Veracruz. Most of the others were little more than local bandits. The royalists began to relax, confident that New Spain was under control again.

But the uprising had not been completely stamped out. It continued to sputter along, and in April 1817 it flared up dramatically when a new revolutionary leader arrived on the scene. Surprisingly, he was a peninsular, born and raised in Spain. His name was Francisco Xavier Mina.

Mina was a liberal thinker who had spent time in England, enthusiastically soaking up progressive ideas. He became filled with a passionate desire to bring liberty and republican government to New Spain. With a small group of followers from Europe, England, and the United States, he landed on the shore of the Gulf of Mexico and marched inland. Although at first he won some battles against local royalist garrisons, Mina did not receive the support he had hoped for from the rebel chieftains of the region, who viewed him with suspicion. He was captured by the royalists and executed in November 1817. At this point it seemed that the revolution had truly run out of steam.

While Mexico was occupied with the wars for independence, Spain was undergoing political convulsions of its own. And as always, events in the parent country caused reactions in the colony. In the parts of Spain that remained free of French control, juntas were formed to manage local affairs until King Ferdinand was able to resume his rule. Together the members of these juntas began to discuss Spain's future. Many of them did not want to return to an absolute monarchy in which the king had complete control; instead, they felt that Spain needed a constitution. A large meeting called the Cortes was held in the Spanish city of Cádiz in 1812. There representatives from the entire Spanish empire, including Mexico, met to write such a constitution. The document they produced was a liberal one. It guaranteed rights such as freedom of speech and of the press to all citizens of the empire. Although the constitution did not allow for the colonies' complete independence, it did say that each colony would become a self-governing dominion within the empire. The Cortes agreed that if and when the French invaders were driven out and the imprisoned Ferdinand returned to power, the king would have to swear to abide by the constitution.

Napoleon Bonaparte was overthrown by an alliance of European states in 1814, and the French threat to Spain ended. King Ferdinand VII swore to uphold the constitution of 1812 and returned to his throne. Liberals in Spain and Mexico rejoiced to see their constitution accepted, and ultra-conservative monarchists were disgruntled. Peninsulares and other conservatives in Mexico fretted that the new liberal trend in Spain would encourage Mexican radicals to demand further reforms.

They need not have worried. Ferdinand had no intention of keeping his word. As soon as he was firmly restored to the throne he mustered support from reactionaries and cancelled the constitution of 1812. The liberals who had written the constitution were jailed or driven into exile. The Spanish Inquisition's age-old powers to repress free thought were restored, and Spain was once again an absolute monarchy.

In Mexico it was suddenly as though nothing had changed since 1808. Juntas that had enjoyed considerable freedom in governing their towns and districts for half a dozen years were abolished, and freedom of speech and of the press no longer existed. The liberals were outraged, and even the conservative criollos, who had grown used to civil rights and a measure of independence from Spanish meddling, were angry. The peninsulares, meanwhile, congratulated themselves on the return of what they believed was the proper order of things. As historian Lesley Byrd Simpson wrote in *Many Mexicos*, "The gachupines were in the saddle and meant to stay there. They had learned nothing from the insurrection."

But although it appeared on the surface that New Spain had returned to its pre-revolutionary condition, the five-year war for independence had brought about profound changes in Mexico. The oppressed and forgotten Indians had tasted their own power. The masses of peasant laborers had been urged to dream of owning their own land. And the revolutionary criollos had learned that they could challenge the royalists on the battlefield.

After Ferdinand's return to the Spanish throne, Mexican society was more deeply divided than ever. At the two extremes were the ultraroyalist peninsulares who wanted the absolute monarchy to continue unchanged and the remaining insurgents who kept the spark of revolution alive and called for a new order. Many people held positions between these two extremes: radicals wanted independence but did not openly ally themselves with the remnants of Hidalgo's revolt; liberal intellectuals wanted to see the Cádiz constitution of 1812 restored; and conservative criollos supported the king but still felt that Mexico deserved better treatment from the parent country.

By 1820, Calleja had retired to Spain and Juan Ruiz de Apodaca had been named viceroy. Apodaca had offered amnesty to the remaining insurgents, believing that it was better to let them turn themselves in without fear of punishment than to prolong the last stages of the revolt. Many of the rebels accepted Apodaca's order and laid down their arms. But Vicente Guerrero and Guadalupe Victoria, with their dwindling bands of guerrilleros, were still carrying on the fight. And in that year Spain's politics once again took a sudden and dramatic twist, this time setting the stage for Mexico to gain its independence at last.

CHAPTER THREE NOTES

p. 32   "I thought that no land . . ." Time-Life Books, *Aztecs: Reign of Blood and Splendor*, Alexandria, 1992, p. 9.

p. 33   "precious as jade." Time-Life Books, *Aztecs: Reign of Blood and Splendor*, p. 25.

p. 35   "The gachupines were in the saddle . . ." Lesley Byrd Simpson, *Many Mexicos* (Berkeley, Calif.: Univ. of California Press, 1966) p. 224.

EMPEROR AGUSTÍN

Spain was seething with discontent at King Ferdinand's tyrannical rule. Many of the discontented were soldiers, angry because the king was reducing the size of the armed forces. Early in 1820 an army of about 14,000 was ordered to Cádiz; these soldiers were supposed to be sent to South America to fight insurgents in the Spanish provinces there. Before they could board their ships, however, their grievances erupted into a revolt. Colonel Rafael Riego led his troops toward Madrid to overthrow the reactionary government, and thousands more joined the march. Spanish liberals and radicals came out of hiding and joyously proclaimed the return of the constitution of 1812.

Confronted with a coup d'état, Ferdinand gave in without a fight. He dismissed the reactionary, repressive ministers he had appointed to important posts in his government, and he humbly promised—for the second time—to uphold the 1812 constitution. Once again Spain's political atmosphere had shifted almost overnight: The conservatives were out, and the liberals were in. The new government immediately began passing progressive laws aimed at reforming Spanish society and loosening the bonds of tradition. But the liberals had been foolishly optimistic to believe Ferdinand's second promise. Less than three years later he broke his word again. With the help of a French army he overturned the constitution and imposed a reign of terror on the liberals. Ferdinand ruled as a tyrant until his death in 1833. Long before that time, however, New Spain had cut its ties with the parent country.

When word of the liberal coup in Spain reached Mexico, the royalists were horrified. Peninsulares, conservative criollos, and high-ranking church officials feared that the liberal reforms might be extended to New Spain, and they agreed that they did not want their longstanding privileges to be taken away by a bunch of Spanish radicals. So they underwent an amazing change of heart. After years of fiercely battling the independence movement, Mexico's reactionary ultraconservatives began to call for independence. They felt they had a better chance of controlling their fates if Mexico stood alone than if it remained tied to a reformist government in Spain. For once the revolutionaries and the reactionaries wanted the same thing.

But the reactionaries and the rebels did not automatically become allies. The ultimate goals of the two groups were very different. The liberals wanted to reshape the social order along democratic lines; the independence-minded conservatives wanted to preserve the traditional order. As a result, the viceregal militia and the guerrilleros continued to snipe at one another. Vicente Guerrero's band of insurgents was still causing trouble in the southern mountains, and in November 1820 Viceroy Apodaca sent a detachment of troops south to deal with this nuisance. To command the mission he chose Agustín de Iturbide, the officer who had captured Matamoros at Valladolid.

Iturbide was only 37 years old at the time, but his career was already a checkered one. Like Morelos, he was born in Valladolid, but he came from a wealthy, aristocratic family. From an early age he dreamed of a military career, and he joined the militia as an ensign at the age of 14. In 1809, when antigovernment plots and radical conspiracies were springing up all over Mexico, Iturbide learned of a plot in Valladolid and promptly informed the authorities. An unhesitating royalist who viewed the Grito de Dolores with alarm, Iturbide was sure that Hidalgo's plans would produce "only disorder, massacre, and devastation." As he explained it, "The word insurrection in that instance did not mean independence and equal liberty;—its object was, not to reclaim the rights of the nation, but to exterminate all the Europeans, to destroy their possessions, and to trample on the laws of war, humanity, and religion." This dark view of the revolution was shared by most criollos.

During the war for independence Iturbide fought valiantly on the royalist side and was promoted to the rank of colonel. As a reward for his good battle record, Viceroy Calleja made Iturbide military commander of a large district in 1815. Soon, however, the viceroy received many complaints from the people of Iturbide's district, who claimed that the commander extorted money from them by force. Although Iturbide was not discharged from the army, he was removed from his command in 1816. Nursing a grudge against Calleja's administration, he took up residence in Mexico City.

Four years later, casting around for someone to bring Guerrero under control at last, Viceroy Apodaca remembered the colonel who had been so brave in battle. Iturbide had been following political events in Spain and Mexico with keen interest. These turbulent events, he later said, "filled the heart of every good patriot with the desire of independence . . . and the apprehension that all the horrors of the former insurrection were to be repeated." Like many other conservative criollos, Iturbide became convinced that Mexico must cut itself loose from Spain. The best way to do that, he reasoned, was to join what remained of the revolution—and then take it over. Only by becoming the new leaders of the revolution could Mexico's wealthy elite preserve their power.

Iturbide formed a bold plan. Following the viceroy's orders, he led a detachment of 2,500 men south to a confrontation with Guerrero, who had kept the flame of the revolution burning for five years since Morelos's death. The two met at the town of Iguala. But instead of attacking the rebel leader, Iturbide invited him to a parley and proposed that they should join forces and liberate Mexico together.

Some historians have said that it was unwise of Guerrero to take a proven turncoat as an ally. But Guerrero had been fighting a long, lonely battle with shrinking support. He knew that his guerrilleros could not long stand up to Iturbide if they came to battle. So after a series of meetings he agreed to merge his army with Iturbide's. Their goal was to establish an independent, unified Mexican nation. First, however, they needed a statement of their plan to publish, so that people would know what they were doing and why. Just as Morelos had produced a set of principles at Chilpancingo, Iturbide produced a similar document at Iguala. It was called the Plan of Iguala, and it appeared in February 1821.

The Plan of Iguala did two things: It declared that Mexico was an independent nation, and it set forth the principles by which that nation was to be governed. Iturbide faced a difficult job in writing the Plan of Iguala, because he wanted to win support from a number of groups that had been bitter enemies of one another in the past: the church, the army, the rebel guerrilleros, the liberal intellectuals, the conservative criollo elite, and the peninsulares. He succeeded brilliantly in devising a plan that gave each group something it wanted.

The Plan of Iguala said that the Roman Catholic church would be the state church of Mexico and that the privileges and dignity of the church and its officials would not be threatened; this pleased the clergy. The army would be responsible for making sure that the plan was enforced; this pleased the soldiers, who did not want the army to lose importance after the revolution was over (Iturbide had very strong support among soldiers, who liked him because he was a lifelong military man). The plan insisted on independence, which pleased the rebels who had been fighting so long for this goal. It called for a congress of representatives elected by the people to make the nation's laws, which pleased the liberal intellectuals. But although the new nation was to have a congress and a constitution, it would not be a republic. It would be an empire, with all the traditional trappings of royalty, which pleased the conservatives. The throne of the new empire would be offered to Ferdinand of Spain; if he did not want it, he could choose another Catholic European prince to become the Mexican emperor. Finally, to reassure those peninsulares who wanted to stay in Mexico, the plan said that criollos and peninsulares would have equal rights in the new nation—earlier, both Hidalgo and Morelos had threatened to confiscate the peninsulares' property and drive them out of the country.

The Plan of Iguala brought together all the quarreling factions within Mexico. Each group decided to join the others in overturning the viceregal government. But this unity was to prove short-lived. The Plan of Iguala only papered over the old rivalries and mistrusts between the various parties; it did not heal them. Furthermore, one very large group in the population was almost entirely neglected in the plan. The Native American people of Mexico had been the heart and the backbone of Hidalgo's 1810 uprising, but in the years since then the question of rights and reforms for the Indian population had faded from the forefront of the revolution. Now, with upper-class criollos taking over the leadership of the revolution, the Indians were ignored by everyone except a few of the original rebels. The Plan of Iguala did protect the Indians from slavery, but it did not mention land reform.

The Plan of Iguala shaped Mexico's political history in two ways. First, it set a pattern for future revolutionaries to follow. From then on everyone who opposed the government began, like Iturbide, by announcing a plan. Publishing a plan came to be seen as an essential first step for every power shift and revolution. The second lasting legacy of the Plan of Iguala was that it placed the army squarely in the center of power. By making the army, rather than congress or the courts, responsible for upholding and protecting the peoples' rights, Iturbide paved the way for military leaders like himself to overturn the government whenever they disagreed with its actions. For years to come the army was to be not only Mexico's defense against other countries but also the most powerful force in its internal government.

But in 1821 the Plan of Iguala seemed to many people to be the only acceptable road to independence. Vows of allegiance to the plan came from rebels, royalists, clergymen, and landowners. Many soldiers immediately became *iturbidistas*, switching their loyalties from the viceroy to Iturbide. One of the first to do so was the commander of a garrison at Veracruz, a young captain named Antonio López de Santa Anna, who was destined to play a major role in the history of both Mexico and the United States.

Viceroy Apodaca refused to accept the Plan of Iguala, but enthusiasm for Iturbide was sweeping through Mexico and the viceroy could do nothing to halt it. Under pressure from his own soldiers, most of whom now leaned toward Iturbide, Apodaca resigned in July 1821. He was replaced by Juan de O'Donojú, who soon saw that Mexican independence was inevitable. Nearly everyone in New Spain—even the one-time loyalists—supported Iturbide. Spain was already struggling to suppress freedom fighters and revolutionary armies in several other American colonies, and it was also weakened by internal bickering. It simply could not muster up the necessary strength to defend its claim on Mexico by force. So O'Donojú decided to give in gracefully. In August he met with Iturbide in the town of Córdoba, and the two men signed a treaty that liberated Mexico.

The terms of the treaty were those that Iturbide had outlined in the Plan of Iguala. First and most important, the treaty guaranteed Mexico's status as an independent state, free to write its own constitution and shape its own future. As Spain's official representative, O'Donojú reluctantly accepted this necessity. From his point of view, the only bright spot in the picture was that the position of emperor in the new Mexico was going to be offered to King Ferdinand. The emperor's power was supposed to be severely limited by the constitution and congress; he would be more of a figurehead than a real force in the new nation's government. But at least with Ferdinand as its head of state, Mexico would continue to be part of the Spanish world.

O'Donojú had not reckoned with Ferdinand's stubbornness, however. The king angrily rejected the Treaty of Córdoba, saying that he had most certainly *not* agreed to let Mexico become independent. Yet there was little Ferdinand could do. The treaty was signed, and his other political troubles prevented him from invading Mexico. The king's rejection of the treaty had one very important effect: Ferdinand could not very well serve as emperor of a nation that he refused to admit even existed. Nor would he agree to let any other European prince take the throne of Mexico. Iturbide, who was both cunning and ambitious, had foreseen this problem. He had insisted on a clause in the treaty that said that if no suitable European prince could be found, the Mexican congress could start a brand-new royal dynasty in the Americas, choosing its own emperor from among the criollos. And if the Mexicans *were* called upon to make such a choice, who would make a better emperor than himself, El Libertador ("the Liberator"), the brave army officer who had brought the war of independence to its triumphant conclusion?

But imperial glory was still just a grand daydream when, after signing the Treaty of Córdoba, Iturbide paraded triumphantly into Mexico City at the head of his army. No one opposed him. The final overthrow of Spanish domination has sometimes been called "a bloodless revolution"

Agustín de Iturbide receives the key to Mexico City upon entering the capital in triumph on September 27, 1821. Having negotiated Mexico's independence from Spain, the ambitious Iturbide quickly made himself emperor of the new nation—but his reign was brief. (Library of Congress)

because Iturbide and his followers did very little actual fighting. But the war of independence was far from bloodless in its early days. Between September 16, 1810, when Father Hidalgo raised the Grito de Dolores, and the September day in 1821 when Vicente Guerrero led his ragged men down out of the hills to march toward the capital at Iturbide's side, much blood was shed by rebels and royalists alike. Many of the victims came from the ranks of Mexico's poor and uneducated Indians and mestizos, who had sought a better life either by joining the revolution or by enlisting in the militia. Thousands died on both sides to set the stage for Iturbide's "bloodless" victory.

Iturbide entered Mexico City on his birthday, September 27. His triumphal entry had all the glamour of a royal procession. Crowds cheered as the mingled armies of Iturbide and Guerrero marched past. The city council presented Iturbide with a golden key to the city upon a silver platter. The archbishop ordered a special mass in honor of the liberator. The city's chief newspaper reported excitedly that such splendor had not been seen since the days of ancient Rome.

Mexico was free, but now it needed a government. Messengers were sent to Spain to offer Mexico's imperial crown to King Ferdinand. In the meantime, the Plan of Iguala said, a small committee would be appointed to act as the regency—the representative of the monarchy—until the emperor was formally crowned. Iturbide appointed the members of the regency, choosing them from among his conservative criollo friends. The regency, not surprisingly, made Iturbide its president.

The regency was only one arm of the new government. The other arm was the congress, with representatives chosen by town and district councils across the country. Because these councils were dominated by conservative criollos, the congress that assembled in the spring of 1822 had a conservative majority. But it also contained some very outspoken liberals. From the start, the congressional conservatives, who wanted to enforce law and order with a strong hand now that the fight for independence was over, clashed with the liberals, who wanted to extend revolution into the area of social reform.

Just about the only thing that everyone in the congress agreed on was the need for more money. Mexico was broke. For years the peninsulares and rich criollos had been sending their money to England and Europe to be invested in banks and industries there, rather than putting it to work in Mexico. The people of Mexico had been paying taxes for centuries, of course—but all that remained of those taxes was in the treasury of Spain. And many of the country's most profitable gold and silver mines had closed down during Hidalgo's revolt and had never reopened during the years of trouble that followed. The new government expected to fill its empty pockets through new taxes, but in the meantime the congress looked for ways to cut expenses. It decided on a drastic money-saving step: reducing the size of the army.

This decision was very poorly received by the soldiers, who left their barracks to roam the street in large, angry gangs. Then Mexico received some bad news from Spain. King Ferdinand had contemptuously rejected both the Treaty of Córdoba and the throne of Mexico. According to the treaty, the Mexicans were now free to elect their own monarch. The soldiers left no doubt in anyone's mind about their choice. On the night of May 18 a sergeant from Iturbide's former regiment gathered a crowd of iturbidistas in a street in downtown Mexico City and began yelling "Emperor Agustín! Emperor Agustín!" Enthusiastically firing their muskets into the air, the mob pressed through the streets to Iturbide's home. More soldiers—and civilian iturbidistas as well—streamed in from all quarters to shout up at Iturbide's balcony, urging him to accept the crown of Mexico. Iturbide later said that he was utterly surprised by this sudden appeal. He added modestly that, although he did not really want to become emperor, he felt that he had a duty to follow the wishes of the people. But most historians agree that Iturbide had probably arranged the whole demonstration with his old sergeant.

The next day, after much heated argument between Iturbide's supporters and those who feared that he was becoming a military dictator, the congress offered Iturbide the throne. He accepted. On May 21 he swore an oath of loyalty to the imperial government and became Emperor Agustín I of Mexico. While the bells were still ringing to celebrate this happy event, Agustín announced that his official coronation ceremony would take place on July 21. Preparations for that ceremony were elaborate and costly. Agustín was determined that his magnificence would rival that of Napoleon Bonaparte, who had crowned himself emperor of France, and every other European head of state. He sent to France for the baroness who had designed Napoleon's uniforms and had her create a host of colorful costumes in silk and satin for himself and the members of his family and court—all of whom were granted flowery titles. To the disgust of the liberals in congress, the imperial court spent hours practicing their bows and curtsies and designing new gold coins with the emperor's portrait on them. The Indian peasants from the countryside got to participate in the festivities, too: They were brought in to scrub the streets and decorate them with flowers and banners for the emperor's parade.

The great day came at last and Agustín I received his crown. He was the emperor of a country that stretched from California almost to South America. In addition to the former colony of New Spain, the Mexican Empire included the Spanish province of Guatemala, consisting of the present-day countries of Honduras, Nicaragua, Guatemala, El Salvador, Belize, and Costa Rica—all of Central America except Panama. Guatemala had won its independence at about the same time as Mexico and joined the new empire at Iturbide's insistence, but the union did not last long. Central America broke away from the empire in 1823. But by then Iturbide was fully occupied with troubles of his own in Mexico.

The emperor won one diplomatic victory soon after his coronation. Mexico wanted to be on good terms with the United States, its northern neighbor, for two reasons. First, because the United States was rapidly expanding westward and the border between the two countries was not yet settled, Mexico worried about its vast northern territories being gobbled up by the United States. Second, Mexico hoped to bolster its sagging economy with loans and investments from the United States. Therefore Iturbide was very eager to gain recognition from the U.S. government. But U.S. president James Monroe was not pleased to see a new monarchy take root in the Americas; he had hoped that all of the newly independent Spanish American lands would adopt republican governments like that of the United States. Finally, however, he did grant recognition to Mexico, and he sent Joel R. Poinsett of South Carolina to Mexico City as the U.S. ambassador.

Poinsett did not think much of Emperor Agustín. A few years later he wrote an account of his visit to Mexico in which he described Iturbide in harsh terms:

I will not repeat the tales I hear daily of the character and conduct of this man. . . . He is accused of having been the most cruel and blood-thirsty persecutor of the Patriots [the followers of Hidalgo and Morelos], and never to have spared a prisoner. . . . In the interval between the defeat of the patriot cause and the last revolution, he resided in the capital, and in a society not remarkable for strict morals, he was distinguished for his immorality. . . . To judge from Iturbide's public papers, I do not think him a man of talents. He is prompt, bold and decisive, and not scrupulous about the means he employs to obtain his ends.

Poinsett believed that the empire might not last long. He speculated that the man who had risen so rapidly to the throne might fall just as rapidly.

Emperor Agustín's position was indeed shaky. Each month his government was spending far more than it was earning, making up the difference with loans from moneylenders at very high rates of interest and thus saddling the young nation with a heavy burden of future debt. Food prices kept rising, and many people could not find work. The lower classes grew increasingly restless. Many of the poorer Mexicans had believed that once Mexico was independent an era of prosperity would set in and they would be better off than ever before. Instead they found conditions as bad as ever, or worse. Among the upper classes, the liberals were furious because Iturbide showed little regard for civil rights. When newspapers ran cartoons and articles that criticized or made fun of him, he shut them down. Guadalupe Victoria, the rebel leader who had been one of Morelos's companions in arms, denounced Iturbide as a tyrant, and several liberal leaders spoke passionately against Iturbide in congress. Even some of the conservative criollos began to grumble that the emperor was going too far. And as feeling against Iturbide grew, he took ever more severe measures against his critics. In August 1822 he arrested members of congress who had publicly criticized his actions, and in October he dismissed the entire congress.

Iturbide's high-handed dismissal of congress turned the country against its sovereign. Iturbide's own career had shown that an army officer with a loyal following could topple a government, and now another young officer planned to do just that. Antonio López de Santa

Anna decided to bring down the emperor. He led his soldiers through the streets of Veracruz, shouting, "Down with Agustín!" Other army officers joined the antimonarchist movement, and so did Guadalupe Victoria and Vicente Guerrero. In February 1823 the antimonarchists gathered in the little town of Casa Mata to issue their revolutionary plan. The Plan of Casa Mata called for a new form of government—a republic rather than a monarchy.

One after another, military units and provincial governors declared their loyalty to the Plan of Casa Mata. A growing army marched toward Mexico City to pull Emperor Agustín from his throne. No fighting was necessary. Iturbide resigned the throne in March and left for exile in Italy. The leaders of the revolt formed a junta, and the work of assembling a congress and writing a constitution began for the second time in less than two years.

As for the former emperor, he could have lived out his life in luxury in Europe, but he was not satisfied with such a tame existence. In early 1824 he wrote to the new Mexican congress offering his services to the nation. "My sole object," he wrote, "is to contribute by my voice and my pen to the support of the liberty and the independence of Mexico." Congress hastily wrote back that it did not need his services and that he if set foot on Mexican soil he would be executed as a traitor. But Iturbide's impatience was to be the death of him. He set out for Mexico without waiting for the reply from congress. Somewhere in the Atlantic Ocean the ship carrying congress's warning to Iturbide passed the ship carrying Iturbide back to Mexico.

Iturbide landed in Mexico on July 12, 1824. He was immediately seized by the local garrison, and one week later he was shot. His last words were said to be, "Fellow Mexicans, in the moment of my death I recommend to you the love of our country and the observance of our holy religion. . . . I die happy, for I die among you!" Mexico's first experiment with a monarchy was over. Now the new republic had to learn how to govern itself.

CHAPTER FOUR NOTES

pp. 38–39 "The word insurrection . . ." An autobiographical sketch by Iturbide, originally published in 1824 and quoted in William

Spence Robertson, *Rise of the Spanish-American Republics As Told in the Lives of Their Liberators* (New York: Collier, 1961), p. 117.

p. 39   "filled the heart . . ." Robertson, p. 119.

p. 47   "I will not repeat . . ." Joel R. Poinsett, *Notes on Mexico Made in the Autumn of 1822, Accompanied by an Historical Sketch of the Revolution* (New York: Praeger, 1969), pp. 68-69.

p. 48   "My sole object . . ." Robertson, p. 137.

p. 48   "Fellow Mexicans, . . ." Simpson, p. 229.

THE MEXICAN REPUBLIC

The war for independence had taken a heavy toll on the country. As many as half a million people—one-twelfth of the country's population—were killed in the wars between 1810 and 1823. Many thousands more were left crippled, orphaned, or homeless. Farms were trampled or burned, mines flooded or abandoned, and roads destroyed. The young republic faced a big task of rebuilding. Tragically, although Mexico had gained independence, the newfound liberty did not bring with it a sense of national unity. The country's population still consisted of many separate groups that felt hostile and resentful toward one other.

Most people in the early republic lived just as they had done for centuries under the colonial system. This was especially true of the Native Americans, who made up more than one-third of the population. Many of the Indians lived in small, traditional Indian villages called pueblos. Some were craftspeople, but most worked the land. They labored on the nearby latifundia of the wealthy estate-owners; they also grew corn, beans, peppers, and melons for their own use on communal village farms called *ejidos* or on tiny individual garden plots called *milpas*. Few of the pueblos had churches, and almost none had schools. Spanish was not spoken, and white faces were very rare.

A laundry in 19th-century Mexico City. The capital was full of people from the countryside—many of them Indians like these women—who flocked to the city in search of whatever work they could find. (Library of Congress)

Other Indians left the pueblos for the rural towns and larger provincial capitals, or even for Mexico City. These Indians mingled with the mestizo population, spoke Spanish, and adopted Spanish-style clothing and customs. They found work as servants, porters (carrying loads of freight on their backs), vendors, craftspeople, military volunteers, and—when industry began to grow—as workers in textile mills and other factories. Town-dwelling Indians often fell victim to the *leva*, a system of forced military draft that allowed local commanders to seize men from the streets without warning and assign them to long periods of service. The worst job, however, was in the mines. The tunnels and shafts were hot and stifling; laborers were required to work long days and carry immense loads of ore; and cave-ins were common. The death toll among mine workers was high. Sometimes a worker's widow was given a share of his last load of ore as a pension.

Life in the countryside and the small rural towns was very different from life in Mexico City and the larger provincial capitals. The urban communities had schools, although enrollment was far from universal—in 1842 only 1 percent of the country's population was attending school. The cities also had theaters, bookstores, cathedrals, and shops with goods from around the world. Political discussion was a passion among the educated, and even the uneducated had some awareness of current events. But people in rural districts—white, mestizo, and Indian alike—seldom thought much about the world beyond their own immediate horizons. The idea of belonging to the Mexican nation was alien to most country dwellers, who identified themselves with their town or district rather than with the country as a whole.

In addition to this difference in perspective, there was also a great gulf in wealth. The country's wealth was concentrated in Mexico City, where it was flaunted by the criollo aristocracy. Fanny Calderón de la Barca, an Englishwoman who married a Spanish diplomat, lived with her husband in Mexico City during the early republic. Her letters, later published, contained an account of the sumptuous attire of criollo wives at a party:

> One, for example, would have a scarlet satin petticoat, and over it a pink satin robe, trimmed with scarlet ribbons to match. Another, a short rich blue satin dress, beneath which appeared a purple satin petticoat. . . . All had diamonds and pearls. . . . I did not see one without earrings, necklace, and broach.

Such elegance made a powerful contrast with the horde of *léperos,* or beggars, who inhabited the streets of Mexico City. Some of them were tricksters who pretended to be ill or wounded, but most were genuinely pathetic—blind, diseased, malnourished, maimed, or alcoholic. U.S. minister Joel Poinsett was repelled by the léperos:

> In front of the churches and in the neighborhood of them we saw an unusual number of beggars, and they openly exposed their disgusting sores and deformities to excite our compassion. I observed one among them wrapped in a large white sheet, who, as soon as he perceived that he had attracted my attention, advanced towards me, and unfolding his covering, disclosed his person perfectly naked and covered from head to heel with ulcers. . . . No city in Italy contains so many miserable beggars, and no town in the world so many blind.

The gap between the very rich and the very poor was most visible in Mexico City, but it existed throughout the country and widened as the years went by. In later years the lower classes grew increasingly resentful that a very small percentage of the population controlled nearly all of the country's wealth.

At the moment of its birth, however, the new nation faced an even more grievous problem. It had no experience with democracy, and no experienced leaders other than military leaders. In 1815 the South American liberator Simón Bolívar had lamented that one of the worst abuses of the Spanish colonial system was that it prevented the people of the Americas from learning how to manage their own affairs. This lack of experience affected all levels of society in Mexico. On the lower levels, the common people—Indians and mestizos in both the country and the towns—were almost entirely uneducated. After 300 years of powerlessness, they were accustomed to taking orders from the military, the local officials, and even the church instead of making decisions for themselves. They could express their rage in a violent revolt, but most of them could not change their day-to-day habits of thought. Citizenship and voting were foreign concepts. As a result the lower classes tended to follow the lead of their tribal chieftains, priests, employers, or local officials. It was many years before the peasant masses began to have an awareness of individual political power and responsibility.

At the higher levels of society, however, there was *too much* regard for individual power. The aristocrats were just as unaccustomed as the peasants were to democratic rule; they were used to being in charge, so they fell into the habit of breaking and rewriting the rules of government to suit the whims of whoever had the most followers. There were few orderly changes of government. Instead, heads of state succeeded one another in a dizzying series of presidents, coups d'état, military dictators, resignations, and reinstatements. Each leader thought that he, rather than the constitution or the congress, was the embodiment of nationhood, and therefore each felt justified in doing pretty much whatever he pleased. Mexico had entered the era of *caudillismo,* or rule by military chieftains.

The *caudillo* was a leader who rose to power on the strength of his ability to command personal loyalty from his followers. Nearly all of the caudillos came from military backgrounds. They had charismatic, colorful personalities that grabbed the attention of crowds, and although some of them were illiterate and uneducated, all of them were highly skilled at judging people's moods and reactions. They were good at manipulating crowds with emotional speeches and dramatic gestures, and they rewarded loyalty with bribes, gifts, jobs, and lavish promises. Some caudillos were men of considerable integrity, like Morelos and Guerrero, but many were interested only in furthering their own importance. Caudillismo was not limited to Mexico; most of the former Spanish colonies in America fell into the hands of caudillos, who often succeeded in taking control because they were willing and able to use severe measures to restore order to troubled countries. Juan Perón of Argentina was a 20th-century caudillo; so was Fidel Castro of Cuba. In 19th-century Mexico, outlying districts were dominated by local caudillos, but over the years a number of caudillos achieved national followings and rose to the highest seats of power.

Because Mexico did not have a tradition of civilian self-government, the best-organized body in the country at the time of independence was the army, which immediately became the focus of political power. For decades the army continued to grow, making and unmaking presidents. No president could long remain in office if the army turned against him. And in the years immediately following independence, the army and the civilian population alike turned for leadership to the only heroes they had: the military leaders who had won the war of independence. Guadalupe Victoria, the rebel leader who had marched at Morelos's side, became Mexico's first president in 1824.

Victoria was an honest, well-meaning man, but he was ill-suited to be president of a turbulent young country. The national legislature and the legislatures of the individual states were rocked by conflicts between liberals and conservatives, between those who wanted the states to have a high degree of independence and those who favored a strong central government. In trying to make fair decisions that would satisfy everyone, Victoria often failed to make any decisions at all. The economy also worsened, partly because of the cost of maintaining a 50,000-man army and partly because many citizens evaded paying their taxes. In 1827 Victoria's vice president tried to lead a coup against the president. The coup was thwarted by Santa Anna and Vicente Guerrero, but it was clear that Victoria's days in office were numbered.

The presidential election held in the fall of 1828 turned into an ugly fight over electoral fraud. According to the constitution, the legislatures of Mexico's 19 states were supposed to choose the president and the vice president. The candidates were Manuel Gómez Pedraza, a scholar with conservative leanings, and Vicente Guerrero, the former rebel and war hero. Ten of the 19 legislatures voted for Gómez Pedraza; by law, he should have become president. But the liberals refused to accept Gómez Pedraza. They accused him of using his popularity with the army to browbeat the legislatures into electing him. A liberal revolt sprang up, and Santa Anna lent his support to Guerrero. This brought large numbers of soldiers to Guerrero's side, and finally Gómez Pedraza withdrew in disgust and Guerrero became president, although he was forced to accept a conservative, Anastasio Bustamante, as his vice president. Guerrero promptly promoted Santa Anna to the highest military rank in the land.

Guerrero took office in 1829, but his presidency was short-lived. Almost at once Mexico faced a serious threat. Spain had not yet recognized Mexico's independence, and now the Spanish planned to reconquer their former colony. Guerrero placed the defense of Mexico in Santa Anna's hands. In July 1829 a Spanish force landed on Mexico's east coast, just as Cortés had done 310 years before. The Spanish troops suffered greatly from thirst, heat, and yellow fever, and their misery increased when Santa Anna surrounded them and subjected them to a siege. The Spanish general surrendered ingloriously, and by October the invaders had withdrawn. The victorious Santa Anna was the darling of the public, the savior of his country.

At the same time, the public's anger at Spain was directed toward the remaining peninsulares and their families. The Plan of Iguala had promised that Spaniards who remained in Mexico would have fair and equal treatment, but now they were subjected to severe taxes and violent mob attacks. They hurriedly packed up and left the country. Their departure was a blow to the economy, for the Spaniards were generally prosperous and they took their wealth out of Mexico. Many of the Spaniards were lawyers, doctors, factory-owners, and merchants, and their businesses were not replaced.

One of the weaknesses of Mexico's constitution was that it allowed the president to set aside constitutional law and take on the powers of a dictator during a time of national emergency—and, as Michael C. Meyer and William L. Sherman point out in *The Course of Mexican History*, "The word *emergency* in the nineteenth century came to be interpreted rather loosely." Guerrero had assumed emergency powers during the Spanish invasion, and afterward he was reluctant to give them up. The conservatives, led by Vice President Bustamante, rallied the army's support and overthrew Guerrero in a coup. Bustamante was declared president in 1830. (Santa Anna, who was closely tied to Guerrero, stayed out of this conflict.)

Bustamante's government proved to be repressive and tyrannical. The conservatives shut down newspapers that opposed them and stole money from the meager public treasury. And like the liberals who had preceded them in office, they proved unable to improve the economy or to end the quarreling between factions. But Bustamante's blackest deed concerned the fate of Vicente Guerrero. After being thrown out of office, Guerrero had fled to his old guerrilla stronghold in southern Mexico. From there he tried to leave the country. He booked passage on an Italian ship, but the captain treacherously accepted a bribe of 50,000 gold pesos from the Bustamante government. When Guerrero boarded the ship the captain seized and bound him, then turned him over to the authorities. He was convicted of treason and shot in January 1831. Four leaders of the war for independence—Hidalgo, Morelos, Iturbide, and now Guerrero—had been executed by their countrymen.

With this execution Bustamante had gone too far. The mood of the country swung against him. From Manga de Clavo, his estate near Veracruz, Santa Anna announced that he was rejecting the Bustamante government. Santa Anna gave his support to Gómez Pedraza, who although he was fundamentally conservative, was a *moderado*—someone with moderate views, willing to seek a middle ground of compromise and balance. Santa Anna's announcement threw the army against Bustamante, who left office for the first time; Bustamante was to hold the presidency twice more in the years to come. Gómez Pedraza was made temporary president until the next elections could be held. No one was in any doubt about who would win those elections. General Santa Anna, who was now called the Savior of His Country, the Conqueror of the Spanish, and the Benefactor of the Fatherland, had let it be known that he would be willing to serve as president if his country wanted him.

When the state legislatures voted in 1833, the 39-year-old Santa Anna was named president by a huge majority. His vice president was Valentín Gómez Farías, a liberal intellectual. The liberal members of congress and the public heaved a sigh of relief and sat back to enjoy the sweeping liberal reforms they expected the new government to enact. But instead of a hoped-for era of stability and reform, they watched the curtain go up on a generation of chaos. Between 1833 and 1855, the presidency changed hands 36 times, and not once was the change the result of a scheduled election. The average term of office was less than eight months. Caudillos mounted coups d'état, presidents resigned and then changed their minds, and the outlines of liberal and conservative ideals became blurred in the whirl of revolts and coun-terrevolts, contending parties, and shifting alliances.

Santa Anna was largely to blame for this state of chaos, for he kept moving into and out of power as the mood seized him. He was president 11 times, although none of his periods in office lasted very long. The problem with Santa Anna was that he was essentially a warrior, not a statesman. He liked the challenge of winning, but he was bored and irritated by the responsibility of serving. Furthermore, he hated being in a position where he had to make decisions and enforce laws, because each decision made an enemy out of whoever disagreed with it, and the driving force in Santa Anna's life was his need to be popular. Just a few months after becoming president in 1833, he retired to Manga de Clavo, claiming that he was in ill health, and left Gómez Farías to deal with the vexing problems of running the country. Santa Anna was to do the same thing on many future occasions; oddly enough, his ill health never kept him from leading an army into battle when called upon to do so. And he was so good at capturing the hearts of the people that even after his unfitness to govern had been demonstrated over and over again, he was able to keep coming back into power.

After Santa Anna left the presidency for the first time, Gómez Farías tried to enact the reforms that the liberals expected. But when he tried to limit the privileges of the clergy and the military and to introduce freedom of religion, the outraged conservatives banded together to call for his overthrow. By removing himself from the presidency Santa

WRITERS OF THE YOUNG REPUBLIC

To Mexican intellectuals, the coming of independence and the birth of the Mexican Republic were world-changing events. The excitement of the times found expression in a flood of new poems, novels, and histories by Mexican writers.

Many of these writers were associated with the Academy of San Juan de Letrán, a society of artists and scholars that was formed in Mexico City in 1836. Some members of the academy became leading literary figures in the new Mexico. One of these was Fernando Calderón (1809–49), a liberal whose plays made fun of Santa Anna. Another was Rodríguez Galván, who wrote poems on a variety of subjects. His best-known work is a long poem called *Profecía de Guatimoc* (1839). It examines Mexico's history from the Indians' point of view. Some verses are passionately anti-Spanish:

Nada perdona el bárbaro europeo.
Todo rompel, y tala, y anquila
Con brazo furibundo.
Es su placer en fúnebres desiertos
La ciudades trocar (¡Hazaña honrosa!)
Ve el sueño con desdén, si no reposa
Sobre insepultos muertos.

The barbarous European forgives nothing.
He breaks and he destroys and he annihilates
With a frenzied aim.
He takes pleasure in converting cities
Into desert wastes (Honorable indeed!).
He views sleep with contempt if he cannot rest
On unburied bodies.

Galván's poem demonstrates one of the major trends in Mexican art and scholarship during the early 19th century: a rejection of Spanish culture and values. Mexicans, especially liberal thinkers, felt that they had struggled to throw off Spanish colonial oppression and now had to rid themselves of old-fashioned Spanish ways of thought as well. This anti-Hispanic stance was apparent in the work of some major historians.

Carlos María de Bustamante, Lorenzo de Zavala, and José María Luis Mora—all of whom had lived through and played some part in the events leading up to the birth of the republic—wrote histories from a strongly anti-Hispanic point of view. They claimed that Mexico's wars for independence had been a reaction to centuries of cruelty and oppression by the Spanish. Their work added support to a view of the Spanish conquest of Mexico that is sometimes called the "Black Legend." The Black Legend can be traced all the way back to Bartolomé de Las Casas. Those who adopt this interpretation of history tend to view the Indians as innocent, peaceful children of nature and the Spaniards as inhuman monsters. Certainly the Black Legend had considerable basis in fact. Yet Lucas Alamán pointed out in his five-volume *Historia de Mexico* (1849–52) that it was not the only possible interpretation of the past.

Alamán was the conservative historian who, as a young man, had lived through Hidalgo's uprising and survived the terrible massacre at the Alhóndiga of Guanajuato. The chaotic violence of that period colored his view of the revolution. His history of the conquest and the colonial era takes the view that the Spanish were benefactors, not oppressors. He states, quite accurately, that slavery and human sacrifice were widespread in Mexico before the Spanish came on the scene. He also credits the Spanish with bringing civilization, Christianity, and peace—even though that peace had to be enforced by the sword.

The conflicting interpretations of Alamán on one hand and his liberal colleagues on the other reflected the opposing political philosophies that had been pulling at Mexico, as if in a huge tug-of-war, for many years. Much of modern Mexican literature and scholarship still takes the form of a debate between the liberal and conservative points of view.

Anna had avoided being tainted by the unpopular liberal policies, and now the conservatives turned to him. He led a revolt against his own former vice president, swept into the presidency for the second time, and cancelled Gómez Farías's reforms. Now a new Santa Anna emerged. After years of fighting on the side of liberal causes he became a staunch conservative, a supporter of the Catholic church, and a heavy-handed believer in the need for a strong central government. He ruled as a virtual dictator. His hand-picked congress of conservatives created a new constitution that took many powers away from the individual states and gave them to the central government, and Santa Anna chose caudillos from among his cronies to run the state governments.

For the next 20 years Santa Anna dominated Mexico's government. Whether he was serving as president, handing the presidency over to one of his friends, going into or coming out of "retirement" at Manga de Clavo, being driven out of office in a revolt, or driving out a rival in a counterrevolt—whatever was happening, Santa Anna was at the heart of it. Bustamante, Gómez Farías, and Nicolás Bravo, a hero of the wars of independence, had several stints each as president, and there were others besides, including José Joaquín Herrera, who occupied the presidential office on three occasions. Herrera, who first came to office in 1844, was the first moderado to be president. His moderate government strove valiantly to reduce the country's debt and bring about a sense of unity. Subject to attacks from both liberals *and* conservatives, the Herrera government did not last long. It was Santa Anna who set the nation's course from the mid-1830s to the mid-1850s. And more than once he took to the field of battle against foreign enemies. The most crucial of these conflicts pitted Mexico against the United States, with bitter results for Mexico.

CHAPTER FIVE NOTES

p. 52   "One, for example, would have a scarlet satin petticoat, . . ." Fanny Calderón de la Barca, *Life in Mexico: The Letters of Fanny Calderón de la Barca,* ed. Howard Fisher and Marion Hall Fisher (New York: Doubleday, 1970), pp. 132–33.

p. 52   "In front of the churches . . ." Joel Poinsett, *Notes on Mexico Made in the Autumn of 1822, Accompanied by an Historical Sketch of the Revolution* (New York: Praeger, 1969), p. 73.

p. 56   "The word *emergency* . . ." Meyer and Sherman, p. 316.

p. 58   "Nada perdona el bárbaro . . ." Poem and translation quoted in Michael C. Meyer and William Sherman, *The Course of Mexican History* (New York: Oxford University Press, 1991), p. 367.

WAR WITH THE UNITED STATES

In addition to the hectic state of affairs within its borders, Mexico faced international problems during its early years as a republic. Spain's failed attempt to reconquer Mexico in 1829 was one such problem, but it was insignificant compared with a far more serious threat on the northern border.

In colonial times Spain had worried about protecting the remoter reaches of its Mexican colony from other nations. The Spanish claim stretched far north and east from the border of present-day Mexico into Texas, California, and the lands between. But few Spaniards settled in this region, far from the seat of power in Mexico City. Aside from some religious missions, mostly in California, the northern territories were almost ignored by the Spanish. In the year 1700 there were only 3,000 colonists in Texas. A century later, in 1800, that figure had risen only to 7,000.

Spain wanted to see this frontier district settled, brought under colonization, and integrated into New Spain. If Spaniards and criollos did not want to live there, the colonial administrators decided, they would throw the land open to those who *did* want it. In 1821, just before Mexico achieved independence, the Spanish gave permission for some American families to settle in Texas. After independence the new

An army officer who served as president 11 times, Antonio López de Santa Anna was alternately adored and hated by his fellow Mexicans. He was a caudillo: a charismatic leader who ruled by a combination of personality and military force. (Library of Congress)

Mexican government confirmed that up to 300 families a year could move from the United States into Texas. The settlers had to be Catholic, and they had to agree to learn Spanish and to live under Mexican law.

American homesteaders flocked into Texas. Land there cost only one-tenth as much as land in the United States, and under Mexican law, which favored the creation of huge ranches, the colonists were allowed to purchase vast tracts of land. By 1827 there were 12,000 immigrants from the United States living in Mexico. The rush continued: By 1835 the immigrants in Texas numbered more than 30,000, compared with only 7,800 Mexicans.

The Americans did not live up to their part of the bargain. Few of them bothered to learn Spanish, and many of them were not Catholics. The Mexican government had hoped that the two populations would blend over time, and that the immigrants would eventually be transformed into Mexicans. But this did not happen. Instead, tension rose between the two populations as the Americans grew impatient at the limits of Mexican law. They outnumbered the Mexicans so greatly that they began to talk of ruling themselves. Rebellion was in the air.

Mexico tried to turn the tide of events away from a confrontation. Congress passed laws against further immigration into Texas, but they proved impossible to enforce. The Mexican army garrisons in Texas were strengthened, and many Mexicans were forcibly resettled in Texas to offset the population imbalance. But these measures caused only more anger and frustration on the part of the American Texans. When Santa Anna ousted Gómez Farías and took power into his own hands, the fears of the Texans rose to fever pitch. They were sure that under the new, strongly centralized government they would have no say at all in their futures. Led by Sam Houston, the Texans armed themselves, and in November 1835 they announced that Texas was seceding, or withdrawing, from Mexico to become an independent country. Thus began a chain of bloody and tragic events.

Mexico was not about to let the Texans' revolt go unchallenged. President Santa Anna, the Benefactor of the Fatherland, prepared to march north and smite the Texans. In his autobiography he wrote:

I, as chief executive of the government, zealous in the fulfillment of my duties to my country, declared that I would maintain the territorial integrity whatever the cost. This would make it necessary to initiate a tedious campaign under a capable leader immediately. . . . I took command of the campaign myself, preferring the uncertainties of war to the easy and much coveted life of the palace.

The campaign that Santa Anna undertook was more than merely "tedious" for the thousands of soldiers he led north: It was brutal. The season was against them. They had to march across a barren landscape in the dead of a bitter winter, and scores perished from hunger and cold. But the first few engagements of the war were Mexican victories. In March 1836 Santa Anna arrived at the Texan settlement of San Antonio and found that 150 Texans, commanded by Bill Travis and including Davy Crockett and Jim Bowie, had barricaded themselves in a fortress called the Alamo. The Mexican commander surrounded the Alamo with his large army and waited for several days. When the Texans showed no sign of coming out, Santa Anna ordered his bugler to blow the *degüello*. This was a traditional bugle call that had been used in Spain for centuries; it meant that the next battle was to be to the death, with no mercy to the enemies. The following morning wave after wave of Mexicans assaulted the Alamo. In the face of heavy defensive fire the attackers opened some holes in the walls and carried the battle inside. The Texans fought bravely; all but five of them were killed in battle. Those five were taken prisoner and then, at Santa Anna's order, shot after the battle was over. This ruthless and blood-thirsty act was a dramatic violation of the customs of war among "civilized" nations, and it set the tone for what was to follow.

A few days later, at the town of Goliad, one of Santa Anna's generals, José Urrea, surrounded a band of 365 Texan fighters. The Texans surrendered, believing that they would be treated as prisoners of war. Urrea sent a message to Santa Anna, urging the commander-in-chief to spare the lives of the prisoners, and then turned the prisoners over to an officer named Nicolás de la Portilla. Santa Anna's instructions to Portilla were blunt: "I trust that, in reply to this, you will inform me that public vengeance has been satisfied by the punishment of such detestable delinquents." Portilla was supposed to kill the Texans without delay.

Portilla was in an agony of indecision. Urrea had told him to treat the prisoners well; Santa Anna had ordered him to kill them. He confided in his diary, "What a cruel contrast in these opposite instructions! I spent a restless night." In the end, Portilla decided to obey his senior commander rather than his conscience. His diary entry for March 27 reads:

I assembled the whole garrison and ordered the prisoners, who were still sleeping, to be awakened. . . . The prisoners were divided into three groups and each was placed in the charge of an adequate guard. . . . I gave instructions to these officers to carry out the orders of the supreme government and the commander-in-chief. This was immediately done.

The 365 prisoners were shot, and the rage of the Texans—already fired by the events at the Alamo—knew no bounds. Volunteers and supplies poured in on Houston, and in less than a month he felt strong enough to take on Santa Anna.

The clash occurred on the afternoon of April 21 near the San Jacinto River. Santa Anna was napping in his tent when the drowsy silence was shattered by yells of "Remember the Alamo!" and the Texans swarmed over the Mexican camp. The battle lasted less than half an hour and ended in utter defeat for the Mexicans. Santa Anna escaped by disguising himself in old clothes and fleeing on horseback, but several days later he was captured by the Texans. The angry mob wanted to shoot "Santy Anny," as they called him, but Houston ordered that as a foreign head of state he must be spared. He made Santa Anna sign an order that gave Texas its independence. Santa Anna reluctantly did so and then was sent packing. Texas became an independent republic—the Lone Star Republic—and remained so until 1845, when it was absorbed into the United States.

Back in Mexico, meanwhile, Santa Anna received a cold reception from those who felt he had given up Texas too easily. Congress refused to recognize the independence of the Lone Star Republic, and the wily Santa Anna retired to Manga de Clavo to prepare his own version of events. Santa Anna's account of the war glorified his own early victories. His sword, as he declared in his florid and boastful way, "was the first to descend upon the necks of the rash enemies of the fatherland!" The ultimate defeat he blamed on other officers. Such was Santa Anna's magic that this version of the affair came to be widely accepted.

Soon Mexico faced another threat, this time from France. In 1838 that country demanded that Mexico pay a large sum—600,000 pesos—to cover losses suffered by French citizens who were living in Mexico during the wars of independence and the subsequent revolts. One of the items on France's list of damages was a bill for 800 pesos from a man who owned a pastry shop. He claimed that a gang of rowdy army officers had burst into his shop one night in 1828, locked him in a closet, and eaten all his pastries. This claim struck the newspapers as ridiculous, and they dubbed the conflict that followed the "Pastry War."

Mexico refused to pay, so France blockaded Veracruz with 26 warships. No ships could enter or leave the harbor, one of Mexico's most important commercial ports. After suffering the effects of the blockade for a few months, the Mexicans agreed to pay. To their great indignation, however, they found that the bill now totalled 800,000 pesos: the original 600,000 plus the cost of the blockade! This insult was intolerable. Mexico sent extra troops to Veracruz, the French ships began bombarding a Mexican fort and landing soldiers on the shore, and the country was in an uproar. Who should step forward to take charge but Santa Anna?

He galloped to Veracruz on his famous white horse and joined battle with the French. He succeeded in driving the French back to their ships, but just as they were retreating an artillery shell not only blew Santa Anna's horse out from under him but also shattered his left leg below the knee.

Santa Anna bled profusely and expected to die at any minute. Yet, with his unquenchable sense of drama, he arranged a moving bedside scene, in which his friends and fellow officers sobbed away while he dictated a 15-page deathbed message to the people of Mexico. It ended on a noble note: "I also beg the government of the fatherland to bury me in these same sand dunes, so that my companions in arms may know that this is the battle line I have marked out for them to hold."

After such a touching farewell, it almost seems a shame that Santa Anna did not die. He recovered, however, after his lower leg was amputated, and he enshrined the severed limb in a handsome tomb at Manga de Clavo. Santa Anna never let anyone forget his war injury. Although he learned to walk perfectly well with a wooden or cork leg, he had the habit of limping slightly whenever anyone disagreed with him, to remind people of the sacrifice he had made for the fatherland. Fanny Calderón de la Barca's account of her 1839 meeting with Santa Anna shows that he was not shy about mentioning his lost limb:

In a little while entered General Santa Anna himself; a gentlemanly, good-looking, quietly-dressed, rather melancholy-looking person, with one leg, apparently somewhat of an invalid, and to us the most interesting person in the group. . . . Knowing nothing of his history, one would have said a philosopher, living in dignified retirement. . . . It was only now and then that the expression of his eyes was startling, especially when he spoke of his leg, which is cut off at the knee. He speaks of it frequently.

MAYA MARVELS REVEALED

In the years 1839–42, while Santa Anna was bouncing in and out of the presidency and tension was building toward war with the United States, an American lawyer and an English artist made two remarkable journeys in southern Mexico. The books they wrote about these trips revealed to the world the splendor of a forgotten part of Mexico's ancient heritage.

A Native American people called the Maya had lived in the Yucatán peninsula of southeastern Mexico, and in nearby Guatemala and Honduras, for thousands of years. But unlike the Aztec people of central Mexico, whose civilization was at its height when the Spanish arrived, the Maya culture had already declined from its peak by the 16th century. The Maya had long since abandoned their immense stone temples and palaces to live as simple farmers, carving out fields from the jungle. They were perhaps the most neglected and overlooked Indians in Mexico.

Since early colonial times people had known that there were ruins half-buried in the jungle in Maya country. One or two determined travelers had even managed to reach them. But these travelers' reports were buried in dusty archives. The world in general had no idea how magnificent the ruins were— and no knowledge of the civilization that had built them. But John Lloyd Stephens, an American lawyer with a taste for travel, had come across one long-forgotten account of the ruins and wanted to know more about them. Together with Frederick Catherwood, an English artist who specialized in drawing ancient ruins, he ventured into the almost entirely unexplored jungles of Honduras in 1839.

The leg itself became a national hero of sorts in 1842, when Santa Anna, during one of his spells as president, had it brought from Manga de Clavo, paraded through the capital, and placed with elaborate honors in an urn at the military cemetery of Mexico City. This was just one of many ways in which Santa Anna indulged his vanity and his love of fancy ceremonies. He filled the streets and parks of Mexico City with

The two men were confronted by fever, mosquitoes, flooded paths, and suspicious Indians. But they doggedly followed their local guides until they reached a vast stone wall, covered with twining vines and dripping moss. It was part of the Maya city of Copán, which flourished from the 5th to the 9th century A.D. As he gazed at the silent stone statues, pyramids, and courtyards that spread in all directions Stephens exclaimed, "America, say the historians, was peopled by savages, but savages never carved these stones." This remark sums up the importance of Stephens and Catherwood's work. They were the first to realize that the Maya ruins were not just the scattered traces of uncultured tribes but the relics of a mighty civilization, with extraordinary building skills and arts that reflected a unique view of the universe. The Maya civilization was every bit as impressive as those of the Aztecs and the Incas, but it was unknown because it had died out centuries before.

Stephens and Catherwood went on to explore other Maya sites at Palenque, Uxmal, and Chichén Itzá in Mexico. Their books *Incidents of Travel in Central America* and *Incidents of Travel in the Yucatán*, brilliantly illustrated by Catherwood, were published in the 1840s and caused a sensation. The books aroused worldwide curiosity about Maya history and culture—curiosity that has not yet been satisfied. Today scientists and scholars from Mexico, Germany, the United States, and other countries are still seeking the answers to many riddles about this ancient civilization. New discoveries are being made all the time in Maya studies, the branch of archaeology that was founded by Stephens and Catherwood.

statues of himself, he ordered artillery salutes to be sounded whenever he went anywhere, and he made his birthday into a national holiday, upon which he was showered with gifts from people wanting favors.

All of this pomp and circumstance weighed heavily on a country that was wracked with discord and hardship. In late 1844 a mob in Mexico City called for the overthrow of the dictator. Angry citizens tore his statues from their pedestals and even went so far as to destroy the sacred leg. With two aides and a cook, Santa Anna fled into the mountains. He was captured and almost killed, but no one quite dared to give the order to execute him, so he was simply sent into exile on one of his estates.

All this time, Mexico had refused to acknowledge the independence of Texas. The problem of the disputed northern border did not go away. It got worse, in fact, when in 1845 Texas became part of the United States. Mexico was furious. Now its neighbor was not merely a small upstart republic but a large and aggressive nation. The Mexican ambassador to Washington, D.C. made a formal complaint and returned to Mexico City. The American ambassador in turn withdrew from Mexico. The two nations were poised for war.

The United States tried to get what it wanted by peaceful means. President James Polk sent an envoy to Mexico City to try to buy the territory that now makes up California and New Mexico; the envoy was authorized to offer $30 million or more. Mexico refused to consider the offer.

By May of 1846 many people in the United States wanted to declare war on Mexico and grab as much territory as possible. But the U.S. secretaries of state and of war argued that such an act of aggression would be illegal. They insisted that they would not allow the country to go to war unless Mexico attacked first. At just that time Polk ordered General Zachary Taylor to lead a detachment of American troops into western Texas to patrol the border. Taylor exceeded his duty, however. He crossed the border and entered Mexican territory, where he got into a skirmish with Mexican troops. Sixteen Americans were killed or wounded. This was all that President Polk and the warmongers in the U.S. Congress needed to hear. Polk made a speech that grossly distorted the facts:

We have tried every effort at reconciliation. . . . But now, after reiterated menaces, Mexico has passed the boundary of the United States, has invaded our territory, and has shed American blood on American soil.

The United States declared war on Mexico, in a thinly disguised land grab, and a large U.S. force began moving toward Mexico by land and sea.

As for Mexico, the country was in a sad state of disarray. With war looming, the people could think of only one savior. They overthrew the current president and invited Santa Anna to return from exile to lead them to victory. He graciously agreed to become president once again. Despite his faults, Santa Anna did have merit as a military organizer and a leader of soldiers. With only 1,839 pesos in the treasury to pay the army, he managed to raise about 18,000 recruits and get them marching northward.

The Americans had taken New Mexico and California with almost no opposition. They easily took the Mexican state of Chihuahua. Then Santa Anna's ragged, starving army of ill-trained recruits met Taylor's army near the town of Buena Vista. The Americans had superior weapons and occupied a superior position, but the Mexicans made a desperate assault that forced the Americans to retreat slightly. Filled with unwarranted confidence, Santa Anna sent a message demanding Taylor's surrender. "Tell Santa Anna to go to hell!" Taylor is said to have exclaimed, but his official response was polite: "I beg leave to say that I decline acceding to your request." In the attack that followed Santa Anna lost 1,500 men. He was forced to withdraw, leaving northeastern Mexico in American hands.

Another U.S. force was attacking by way of Veracruz. General Winfield Scott cut off that city's escape routes and then subjected it to two days of constant heavy mortar bombardment, despite the pleas of foreign consuls that women and children be allowed to leave the beleaguered port. The devastation was terrible. The dead were piled in the streets, and buildings burned on all sides. Veracruz surrendered. Scott had lost 67 men, but 1,500 Mexicans were dead; two-thirds of these were civilians.

Scott marched on Mexico City. Santa Anna tried to halt the Americans, but he was outfought, and the American advance continued. The Mexican defense was weakened by fatal arguments between Santa Anna, the other generals, the congress, and the city council. No one would take overall responsibility, and no group wanted to cooperate with any other. As a result the city fell to the invaders, although some Mexican units fought nobly in isolated engagements. The fiercest and most heroic battle was that of Chapultepec Castle, a fortress overlooking the city that was defended by 1,000 soldiers and the young cadets of the Mexico City Military Academy. Unable to drive the defenders out with artillery fire, Scott ordered a full-scale assault on the castle, the only part of the capital that had not yet fallen. The American soldiers attacked the walls with pickaxes and climbed over them with ladders to wipe out the defenders in hand-to-hand fighting. The cadets held out to the last; legend says that one of them wrapped himself in the Mexican flag and hurtled over the battlements rather than surrender. Today the cadets are honored as the *Niños Héroes,* the Boy Heroes, and every September 13, on the anniversary of the battle, flowers are brought to Chapultepec Castle in a solemn celebration.

Santa Anna, meanwhile, had marched out of the capital without even fighting! He blamed the fall of Mexico City on the "betrayers of the fatherland," a category that seemed to include everyone except himself. In disgrace with his fellow Mexicans, he sought refuge in Oaxaca in the south, but the liberal governor of that state, Benito Juárez, turned him away. The generalissimo was forced to surrender to the Americans. He was again sent into exile, this time in the South American country of Venezuela.

The victorious Americans and the shattered Mexicans signed the Treaty of Guadalupe Hidalgo in February 1848. In return for a payment of $15 million, Mexico officially gave to the United States the territory that now makes up Texas, California, New Mexico, Arizona, Nevada, and parts of Utah and Colorado. The border of Mexico was redrawn at approximately its present location, along the Río Grande. Mexico had given up half its territory, and it was getting only half the amount that the United States had offered to pay in the first place. Ironically, just a few months later gold was discovered in California, but the gold rush that would have been a welcome relief to Mexico's empty treasury went instead to enrich the United States.

The Mexican-American War and the Treaty of Guadalupe Hidalgo left a legacy of frustration and despair in Mexico. Anti-American feeling was strong, but so was a feeling of failure and futility. The Mexican Republic had been in existence for 25 years, and Mexico's problems seemed worse than ever. There was a sense of confusion, too, as people looked for a leader to make things right.

Immediately after the war José Joaquín Herrera's moderate government returned to power. Once again, though, the moderates failed to please a nation that had grown used to extremes. Order was breaking

OREGON
TERRITORY

MISSOURI
TERRITORY

ACQUIRED FROM
MEXICO, 1848

WI

MI

IOWA

OH

IL   IN

MO   KY

TN

INDIAN
TERR.   AR

MS   AL

TEXAS
ANNEXATION
1845   LA

MEXICO

Pacific
Ocean

Mexico City   Veracruz

Mexican Territory Acquired
by the United States, 1848

down throughout the land. States and cities abruptly announced that they were seceding from the republic. Caudillos in every community made and broke new sets of laws almost daily. Corruption was eating away at every level of government. An accused prisoner could bribe a judge for a few pesos; a British agent boasted that he had bribed 35 members of congress for the bargain price of 60,000 pesos. Something had to be done to bring order out of chaos. The troubled nation turned where it had so often turned before—to Santa Anna.

A conservative revolt brought the 60-year-old generalissimo back from Venezuela in 1853 to take the presidency for the 11th and last time. Santa Anna was given the title "Perpetual Dictator," and all pretense at democracy was abandoned. Liberals were driven into hiding or exile. Benito Juárez, the liberal governor who had refused to shelter Santa Anna in Oaxaca after the war, fled the country to New Orleans, where he worked as a cigarette roller to make a living; other liberals skulked in the southern mountains and planned revolts, just as Morelos, Victoria, and Guerrero had once done.

Mexico's final burst of *santanismo*—adoration of Santa Anna—did not last long. The country was tired of him, and he was tired of the country. When a liberal uprising drove him from power in 1855, he did not try to fight it. Instead he took a coach to the coast and returned by sea to his comfortable life in Venezuela. Seventeen years later, old and ill, Santa Anna returned to his homeland. He lived there in silence and obscurity until his death in 1876. By that time the country he once ruled had undergone tremendous changes.

CHAPTER SIX NOTES

p. 64   "I, as chief executive . . ." Santa Anna, Antonio López de, *The Eagle: The Autobiography of Santa Anna*, edited by Ann Fears Crawford, translated by Sam Guyer and James Platón (Austin, Texas: Pemberton, 1967), pp. 49–50.

p. 65   "I trust that . . ." Quoted in Wilfrid H. Callcott, *Santa Anna: The Story of an Enigma Who Once Was Mexico* (Norman, Okla.: University of Oklahoma Press, 1936), p. 133.

p. 65   "What a cruel contrast . . ." Quoted in Carlos E. Castenada, editor and translator, *The Mexican Side of the Texas Revolution* (Dallas: Turner, 1928), p. 236.

p. 65   "I assembled the whole garrison . . ." Castenada, p. 236.

p. 66   "was the first to descend . . ." Quoted in Lesley Byrd Simpson, *Many Mexicos* (Berkeley, Calif.: University of California Press, 1966), p. 241.

p. 69   "America, say the historians, . . ." Anne Ward, *Adventures in Archaeology* (New York: Larousse, 1977), p. 60.

p. 67   "I also beg the government . . ." Simpson, p. 245.

p. 67   "In a little while entered General Santa Anna . . ." Simpson, p. 245.

p. 70   "We have tried every effort . . ." Armin Rappaport, ed. *The War with Mexico: Why Did It Happen?*, (New York: Berkley Books, 1983), p. 6.

p. 71   "Tell Santa Anna . . ." Charles Dufour, *The Mexican War: A Compact History,* (New York: Hawthorn Books, 1968), p. 172.

JUÁREZ AND THE LIBERAL REFORMERS

Among those who had opposed Santa Anna during the generalissimo's final presidency was Juan Alvarez, a veteran of the wars of independence. Alvarez was an old-time guerrilla chieftain in the style of Vicente Guerrero. With suggestions from a group of exiled liberal intellectuals he prepared the Plan of Ayutla, which called for a liberal takeover of the government. The revolt that followed the publication of this plan in 1855 is called the Revolution of Ayutla. It drove Santa Anna out of power for the last time, and it gave the presidency to a series of liberals. The most important of these was Benito Juárez, a towering figure in Mexico's history.

Juárez, a full-blooded Zapotec Indian, was born in 1806 in Oaxaca. When he was 12 years old he left his village for Oaxaca City, where his older sister had found work for him as a servant. Juárez's employer was so impressed with the boy's character and intelligence that he paid for Juárez's education. At his patron's request Juárez entered a seminary and studied to become a priest, but he soon decided that the priesthood was not for him and took up the study of law instead.

In 1831 Juárez received his lawyer's certificate. He worked as a lawyer in Oaxaca City, often defending poor Indians for free. He also

A Native American from Oaxaca state who became a lawyer, rebel leader, and president, Benito Juárez fought tirelessly to reform Mexico's laws and win justice for the poor. (Library of Congress)

served in the city council and, later, the state legislature. Juárez came to believe that the injustice and suffering he saw around him could not be eliminated by lawyers—the laws themselves had to be changed, and the way to do this was through political action. He was elected to the national congress, and then he became governor of Oaxaca state; it was at this time that he denied sanctuary to Santa Anna. Juárez was an honest and efficient governor, but when Santa Anna returned to power in 1853 the vengeful dictator exiled Juárez, who joined a group of Mexican liberals in New Orleans and began to plot the Revolution of Ayutla.

After the Revolution of Ayutla, Alvarez, Juárez, and the other liberals established themselves in Mexico City and began to hammer out a new constitution. But now that they had won power, the liberals could not agree among themselves; they split into several factions. The main split was between moderados such as Ignacio Comonfort, who felt that the liberals should be willing to make some compromises with the conservatives in order to prevent further fighting, and the *puros,* or purists, who intended to transform the country with radical new laws and did not want to compromise. Juárez was a puro. Comonfort came into the presidency, but he found, like Herrera before him, that his moderate position won him no friends, only enemies.

The constitution that was presented to the nation in 1857 pleased the radical liberals and horrified the conservatives, especially the clergy and those who believed that the church's authority should be greater than that of the state. The Constitution of 1857 was deeply anti-clerical; that is, it took the position that the church and clergy did not have special rights and privileges, and it placed the authority of the state above that of the church. The constitution contained a bill of rights that guaranteed all Mexican citizens freedom of speech, of the press, and of assembly, as well as equality under the law. It abolished all aristocratic titles. It also outlawed slavery and compulsory servitude; this provision was supposed to reduce debt peonage, but it also meant that monks, priests, and nuns would now be allowed to leave the church without punishment. Under the new constitution, some property owned by the church and other organizations would be sold at public auctions. The church would also be forced to abandon its practice of charging high fees to perform sacraments—if people wanted religious services and could not pay for them, the priests were required to perform them for free. And although the Constitution of 1857 did not guarantee religious liberty, it also did *not* establish the Roman Catholic church as the state church, which suggested that other religions were to be tolerated.

These insults were more than the church could swallow. Archbishops, bishops, and priests thundered from the pulpit that anyone who swore allegiance to the constitution would be excommunicated (thrown out of the Catholic faith). The many Mexicans who were both patriotic and deeply religious found themselves in a terrible dilemma.

If they failed to uphold the constitution they could be accused of treason; if they supported the constitution they risked eternal damnation. A mood of unrest pervaded the country, fed by the grumbles of the pro-clerical faction. To add to the unrest, Pope Pius IX, head of the worldwide Roman Catholic church, sent a message from Rome urging Mexican Catholics to disregard the constitution. This remarkable document claimed that the pope had the right to interfere in the internal business of any country whenever Catholics' privileges were threatened. It accused Mexico's liberal government of allowing dangerous practices such as free thought:

For the purpose of more easily corrupting manners and propagating the detestable pest of indifference and tearing souls away from our Most Holy Religion, it allows the free exercise of all cults and admits the right of pronouncing in public every kind of thought and opinion.

Mexico was in a state of crisis, its people suddenly forced to choose between their country and their church. Both sides in the dispute ruthlessly used whatever power they had to sway people. Government workers who would not take an oath of allegiance to the constitution were fired. Catholic hospitals turned away sick and injured people who *had* taken the oath, such as soldiers. In 1858 the inevitable revolt broke out. A conservative general named Félix Zuluoga proclaimed his plan, which consisted mainly of discarding the controversial constitution. The army backed Zuluoga and declared him president. Juárez escaped to a rebel stronghold in Querétaro, and there his supporters proclaimed *him* president. Civil war had begun.

The three-year War of the Reform (1858–61) pitted Juárez's liberal government against the Zuluoga administration. Although Zuluoga held Mexico City, the liberals dug themselves in at Veracruz. They used the taxes paid at that port to buy weapons from abroad, with which they armed the liberal forces. Both sides were guilty of merciless deeds, such as shooting captured prisoners. One especially brutal conservative general killed all the doctors in Mexico City who had treated wounded liberals; some liberals, in turn, executed priests and defaced churches. Meanwhile, as always during times of revolution and civil war, armed

PUEBLO LIFE

Throughout the 19th century, many Native Americans in rural Mexico continued to live just as their ancestors had done in colonial times and even earlier. Their traditional ways of life had evolved over the centuries to suit the environment in which they lived.

In the *tierra caliente*, the "hot land" of the south and the coastal lowlands, the Indians built small huts or cottages, using poles for supports and palm leaves for walls and roofs. These homes were airy, cool, and easy to replace after a rainy season. In the cooler and drier parts of the country the Indians built flat-roofed houses of stone or adobe, a kind of brick made of sub-baked earth. The native peoples of Mexico also showed great skill in fashioning arts and crafts from the materials available to them. Some, like the people of Tonala, a village near Guadalajara, were noted for their fine clay pottery; others were famed for woodworking or weaving. The Tarascans of Michoacán state created a craft based on gourds, which were plentiful there—they split and varnished the gourds, often painting them with floral designs, and used them for dishes. These artifacts were highly prized by the few European travelers who visited the Indian pueblos and village markets.

Life in a pueblo was not easy, however. In addition to providing food for their families, many Indians had to work as

bands of marauders roamed the countryside, looting and burning, with no regard for any political philosophy except the philosophy of grabbing what they could while there was no law to restrain them.

By 1860 the war was going in the liberals' favor. Several brilliant liberal generals dealt crushing defeats to Zuluoga's army, and early in 1861 the 25,000-man liberal army marched in triumph into the capital. Juárez was elected president several months later. But the liberals *still* could not agree. This time they argued about punishing the conservatives. Some liberals called for all the conservatives to be executed, but Juárez spared most of his enemies' lives. With the war over, he felt, it laborers on large estates owned by the criollos; they also had to pay taxes. Men usually worked in the fields, but, as Ruth Olivera and Liliane Crete point out in *Life in Mexico under Santa Anna, 1822–1855,* "Indian men and women worked hard, but the woman undoubtedly did the greater part of the work." Women's chores included weaving, fetching water (often from distant wells or streams), and tending the family's pigs and chickens as well as the children. No home was without its *metate,* the grinding stone that was used to grind corn into flour. After grinding the flour, a woman would mix it with water and shape it into a thin sheet that was baked on a *comal,* or clay baking dish. The resulting tortilla was the staple food of the Indians, accompanied by beans, chili peppers, onions, pumpkins, and melons.

Only slowly, as priests and teachers made their presence felt in the pueblos, did life begin to change for Mexico's Native American population. And even today many Indian communities lag behind the rest of the nation in terms of services such as clean water, schools, and medical care. But the issue of Indian rights is no longer callously ignored, as was so often the case in earlier years, and the invisible barrier that used to segregate the large native population has begun to give way. Interest in Native American languages, culture, and arts is at an all-time high among the young people of Mexico, and the pueblo is no longer the limit of the Indian's world.

was time for healing and forgiveness. Mexico was impoverished and in ruins. Juárez faced a massive job of rebuilding. Before he could begin, however, the country was plunged into war again.

Trying to help the ailing treasury, Juárez announced that for the next two years he would not make any payments on Mexico's large debts to foreign countries. This angered the governments of England, France, and Spain, to whom Mexico owed money, and the three nations agreed to send an army of occupation to Mexico to collect the debt. At the beginning of 1862, troops from the three nations landed on the coast at Veracruz, the point of entry for so many invaders over the centuries.

England and Spain really were there simply to force the payment of the debts owed to them, but France had a secret motive. France was now ruled by an emperor, the nephew of Napoleon Bonaparte. This ruler, Napoleon III, planned to invade Mexico and bring it completely under French control. When the British and Spanish commanders learned of this imperialistic plot, they refused to have anything to do with it and took their troops back to Europe. But the French army, bent on conquest, marched toward Mexico City.

At Puebla, a city between the coast and the capital, the French army met resistance from a Mexican army led by some of the liberal commanders who had performed so well in the War of the Reform. The Mexicans' dogged defense not only held Puebla but forced the French to retreat—this victory was partly due to a brave young general named Porfirio Díaz, who would figure prominently in Mexican political life a few years later. The Mexicans were tremendously proud of the Battle of Puebla, and the anniversary of the battle, May 5 or *Cinco de Mayo,* was to become one of Mexico's most festive national holidays.

The French menace did not go away, however. The French army returned and besieged Puebla, cutting off all food and water supplies. After two months the defenders were reduced to eating rats and leaves, and they finally surrendered. The fall of Puebla left the road to Mexico City wide open to the invaders. President Juárez fled the capital, taking his government first to the northern city of San Luis Potosí and then farther north. The French entered Mexico City, where ultraconservatives and the clerical faction—glad to see the liberals on the run— greeted the invaders with flowers and songs.

France wanted to turn Mexico into a Catholic monarchy. Napoleon III and a handful of Mexican conservatives got together to choose a king, and their choice fell on Ferdinand Maximilian, an Austrian archduke (they advised him to use the name Maximilian, as Ferdinand was an unpopular reminder of King Ferdinand VII of Spain). Flattered, Maximilian agreed to become emperor of Mexico. Early in the summer of 1864 he and his young wife arrived at Veracruz. After a rough journey over mountain roads that almost destroyed his elegant European carriage, the archduke reached the capital and was crowned Maximilian I.

Maximilian's Mexican adventure was a mass of confusion from the start. The young emperor believed that the people of Mexico had voted to accept him as their monarch, but in reality the leading conservatives had arranged a fraudulent vote. Many Mexicans were actually seething with anger that their country's hard-won right to rule itself had been usurped by foreigners. Maximilian was neither evil nor tyrannical; in fact, he tried in a feeble way to do a good job. He upheld some of Juárez's liberal laws, hoping to mend the breach between liberals and conservatives, and one day each week he held a sort of open house at the imperial palace, so that anyone who had a grievance or a problem could come and present it before the emperor—most of the time, however, he was unable to do anything to solve the problem. Maximilian also had big plans for Mexico City. He wanted to make the city into a glittering international capital, worthy of comparison with Paris and other European cities. He planned wide boulevards, spacious parks, and a national art gallery. But there was no money in the treasury to finance these schemes. Even worse, Maximilian had no real support outside the conservative elite. His empire was doomed to fall.

Just as Morelos and his followers had once waged guerrilla war against the royalists in the southern mountains, now Juárez and the other liberals became guerrilleros in the north, along the U.S. border. Juárez set up headquarters in the border town of El Paso del Norte; today this town is called Ciudad Juárez (Juárez City). The *juaristas*, as his followers were called, kept the war alive, and the French could not pacify the region. In 1865 the exasperated Maximilian ordered that any juarista caught with a weapon was to be executed. This decree made the liberal rebels even more determined to fight the usurper to the death.

By this time the juaristas were getting some help from the United States. The United States had regarded itself as the policeman of the Americas ever since 1823, when President James Monroe issued the Monroe Doctrine. This doctrine stated that the United States would oppose any attempt by a European nation to meddle in the affairs of an American nation, or any attempt to set up a monarchy in the Americas. As the years passed, many people in Latin America resented the way the United States took upon itself the role of peacekeeper and freely told other nations what to do; their resentment grew quite strong at times in the 20th century. But in the mid-19th century, Juárez and the other liberals were ready to welcome any U.S. weapons and volunteers that might help them drive the imperialistic French out of their country.

During the early years of the French invasion, the American Civil War (1861–65) had kept the United States far too busy with its own affairs to interfere in politics south of the border. But as the Civil War moved toward its close, the United States began to pay attention to the troubles in Mexico. The U.S. government gave weapons and ammunition to the juaristas and allowed them to recruit American soldiers of fortune; nearly 3,000 veterans of the Union army signed up to serve under Juárez.

Back in France, meanwhile, Napoleon III was worried about the growing threat of war with Germany. This threat, combined with the rising strength of the juaristas, made Napoleon summon home his troops in 1866. The French army withdrew, leaving the hapless Maximilian to his fate. The emperor's advisers begged him to retreat to Europe, but he believed there was a chance that he could hold on to his empire. He sent his wife, Carlota, to Europe to beg the pope and other heads of state for help; when this mission failed, the distraught woman went insane, never to recover. By this time Juárez's republicans were on the march.

They came down out of the deserts and highlands of northern Mexico and captured a string of cities, one by one: Monterrey, Durango, Guadalajara, Oaxaca. The Mexican imperial army was unable to stand against them, and indeed many of Maximilian's soldiers, seeing which way the wind was blowing, switched sides and joined the republican army. Maximilian valiantly but foolishly attempted to lead his army in person. He was besieged in the city of Querétaro, and there he surrendered to the republican army in May 1867.

Juárez insisted that the captured emperor face a court-martial in which the main charge would be the murder of Mexican citizens—this was based on the order Maximilian had signed in October 1865 that called for the execution of juarista prisoners. Maximilian's plight aroused the world's sympathy. To many outside Mexico (and some inside) it seemed cruel that he should face death because of a misguided venture that had not even been his own idea. Kings and presidents begged Juárez to be merciful, and so did processions of tearful women who felt sorry for the handsome archduke. But Juárez could not be moved. He wanted to show the world that any violation of Mexico's sovereign right to govern itself was a deadly mistake. He also felt that by showing mercy to his opponents after the War of Reform he had only encouraged them to rise up against him again, and he did not want to make that mistake twice. So when the court-martial

About to go before the firing squad, Maximilian, archduke of Austria and former emperor of Mexico, comforts a distressed priest. The French placed Maximilian on the Mexican throne and then abandoned him to a tragic fate. (Library of Congress)

brought in a verdict of guilty, there was no appeal. On June 19, 1867, Maximilian met death in front of a firing squad at a place called the Hill of Bells outside Querétaro. Mexico's second empire had ended. Carlota, the onetime empress of Mexico, lived on in Europe, secluded and unhappy, for six decades after Maximilian's death.

Juárez now found himself in a position that was occupied by many Mexican heads of state during the 19th century. He was newly restored to leadership over a country that had been ravaged by war upon war, and he somehow had to begin rebuilding industry, trade, agriculture, and—most important—feelings of confidence and security among people who had been terrorized for years. But Juárez never shirked a difficult or even a dangerous duty. He shouldered the burden of leadership, restored the constitution of 1857, and tried once more to enact his beloved liberal reforms. This time he had some success.

Education had always been the privilege of the monied classes. Juárez, who had been lucky enough to go to school purely as the result of someone's generosity, keenly felt that everyone should receive at least a basic education. His new laws made primary school free and compulsory—in other words, all pupils, both boys and girls, were required to attend. But it would be many years before Juárez's dream of universal education could even begin to come true. Schools had to be built, teachers had to be trained, and parents and children alike had to get used to the idea of school. At least, however, he had made a start toward better educational opportunities for all.

Juárez also tried to make a start at land reform, the cherished goal of the Indian peoples whom he had pledged to help. In this he was less successful. Under the constitution, some tracts of land owned by churches and other organizations were to be sold. Juárez may have thought that this would give the landless poor a chance to obtain their own property, but if so he misjudged the effect of the law. For one thing, the land was sold, not given away, and very few peasants had the cash to buy it. For another, the law could be interpreted to require the sale of the ejidos, the traditional communal farms of the Indian villages. Even the Spaniards had respected the ejidos, but under the Constitution of 1857 some of them were broken up and sold. The buyers were not Indians but land-greedy *hacendados,* the owners of the *haciendas,* as the large rural estates were now called. So Juárez's attempt at land reform ended by helping the very hacendados who exploited the labor of Indian and mestizo peons. But although Juárez's reforms did not much improve the lot of the Indians, they did break up some of the church's immense estates.

The biggest successes of the Juárez regime were in economics. Juárez appointed a capable finance minister who drew up a budget and revised some of the tax laws. Juárez and his finance minister wanted to encourage foreign companies to invest in Mexican business, but they knew that Mexico would not attract investors until its entire transportation system was overhauled. Roads throughout the country were rutted, muddy or dusty according to the season, and, worst of all, haunted by bandits. To bring the bandits under control Juárez strengthened the *rurales,* the rural police. Mounted on horseback, with rifles slung over their shoulders and wide-brimmed sombreros shading their eyes from the sun, the rurales became a common sight in the countryside. Some of them were bullies, little more than bandits themselves. Most, however, did a heroic job of making travel in Mexico safer.

Juárez's landmark achievement was bringing Mexico into the age of railways. Iron tracks had swept across the United States, bringing growth and industry to the West. Yet by 1860, when the United States had more than 30,000 miles of railroad tracks, Mexico had only about 150 miles. Freight was carried in oxcarts, on horseback or muleback, and on the backs of *cargadores,* men who worked as load-carriers. Years earlier a British company had begun to build a railway line between Veracruz and Mexico City, but the project had run out of money. Juárez felt that this railway would be of unimaginable benefit to Mexican trade and industry, and he scraped up funds to get it built. The engineers performed miracles. To scale the heights that separated the coast from the central plateau they had to lay track across scores of steep gorges and blast tunnels through dozens of mountains. Finally, in December 1872, the last sections of the track were laid. The railway from Mexico's chief port to its capital city was complete.

Sadly, Juárez did not enjoy this triumph. Amid increasing strife among the liberals and threats of revolts from the provinces, he had died of a stroke the previous July. He was succeeded in office by Sebastián Lerdo de Tejada, who continued the programs of educational and economic reform that Juárez had begun.

The young Benito Juárez might haved seemed an unlikely prospect for glory. Few would have predicted that a poor, illiterate Indian boy, orphaned at the age of three, would become a lawyer, a political philosopher, a statesman, and a skilled leader of men. But it was Juárez's virtues of character that placed him above most other politicians of his era. All of the generals, caudillos, warlords, and party leaders loudly claimed to put the good of their country before their own good—but in Juárez's case it was true. Today he is recognized as one of Mexico's finest patriots.

CHAPTER SEVEN NOTE

p. 71   "For the purpose . . ." Quoted in Lesley Byrd Simpson, *Many Mexicos* (Berkeley, Calif.: University of California Press, 1966), p. 275.

PORFIRIO'S PEACE AND MADERO'S REVOLUTION

Porfirio Díaz—the hero of the Battle of Puebla— had tried once to start a revolt against Benito Juárez. The revolt was unsuccessful, but it was an example of a pattern that appears many times in Mexico's political history: Two men start out as allies in a common cause and then, when their enemy has been overcome, turn against each other. Díaz and Juárez had both fought under the liberal flag against the French, but once Juárez became president, Díaz tried to unseat him. The tendency toward caudillismo remained strong throughout 19th-century Mexico, especially among military leaders like Díaz.

When Juárez died, Díaz wanted to take over as Mexico's leader. He ran for president against Juárez's successor, Lerdo de Tejada, but lost the election. Díaz bided his time during Lerdo's term in office and then, when Lerdo said that he was going to run for a second term as president, Díaz did not wait for the next election. He published a plan that called for revolt. The keystone of Díaz's plan was that no president should be allowed to serve for two terms in a row. He warned that a president who stayed in power for eight years could easily turn into a dictator. Díaz, whose supporters included many soldiers and several capable commanders, marched on the capital. His force met the federal army and defeated it in a single battle. Lerdo sailed into exile, and Díaz took control of Mexico City and the country. He remained in control for the next generation, with one brief interruption.

After his first four-year term as president, Díaz was in an awkward position. Because he had risen to power on the slogan "No Re-election!" he felt he could not run for re-election without openly betraying his own cause. He gave his support to Manuel González, his secretary of war, who was elected president in 1880. During González's term in office Díaz remained active in the government. He served in the presidential cabinet and also acted as a state governor. It was clear that Díaz planned to return to the presidency, and he used his influence to help advance his friends' careers, building up a fund of gratitude for the future. As president, González did nothing to anger Díaz; he knew that Díaz could overthrow him if he chose.

González was an unpopular president. Many officials of his administration were accused of taking bribes and stealing from the treasury, and unsavory stories about González's personal life were whispered around the capital. Díaz easily won the presidential election of 1884. And having returned to power, he did not give up his hold on the presidency again for more than 25 years. Conveniently casting aside his pledge of "No Re-election!" he ran for president in every election, and he made sure that he won. He used the army, the rurales, and gangs of thugs to frighten people into voting for him. When that failed to work he had the vote counts rigged in his favor. Díaz became the dictator that he had warned Mexico against just a few years before.

Mexico, Díaz saw, had become a giant battleground, trampled underfoot by the many factions who were tearing the country apart in their ceaseless struggle for power. He believed that the constant wars and rebellions, as well as the frequent and rapid changes of government, had made Mexico so weak that it was almost beyond hope. Both agriculture and industry were at a standstill, and the country lagged far behind other nations in terms of modern developments such as railways, electric power, and communications systems. Mexico's stormy politics and its backwardness had become something of a joke in the United States and Europe, and this was an insult to national pride—but

Porfirio Díaz, a hero of the war against the French invasion, became president in 1876 and used fraud and force to remain in power until 1911. The Porfiriato—as this period is called—saw many economic improvements in Mexico, but human rights were trampled by the Díaz government. (Library of Congress)

more serious was the fact that foreign companies would not build factories or do business in Mexico until they believed that their investments would be safe from civil unrest.

Díaz was closely advised by a group of criollo lawyers, economists, and scholars who were called the *científicos* because of their faith in science and technology. Like the científicos, Díaz was convinced that Mexico's growth—perhaps even its very survival—depended upon progress. The country needed roads, dams, industries, and better farms in order to feed its people and compete in the international marketplace. Mexico's treasury was empty, and other countries refused to loan Mexico money because they were afraid that they would not be repaid. Foreign investment companies seemed to be Mexico's best hope of getting the things it needed, but such companies were nervous about venturing into a country that was still struggling to find its identity. Díaz determined that a long period of peaceful, stable, orderly rule was needed to settle Mexico's internal troubles and to reassure the rest of the world that Mexico was a safe place. He knew that by using force to stay in office he was violating Mexico's constitution as well as his own earlier liberal beliefs, but he felt it was necessary to do so. He justified his acts by claiming that Mexico was not yet ready to govern itself; it needed a strong hand, he said. He knew what was best for the country, and he would provide the strong hand. The watchwords of his rule would be *Order*, followed by *Progress*.

The period during which Porfirio Díaz controlled Mexico is known to historians as the Porfiriato, the time of Porfirio. But it has also been called the Pax Porfiriana—Latin for "the peace of Porfirio"—for Díaz did succeed in bringing a great measure of order and stability to the land. He increased the number of rurales and used them to patrol highways and quell uprisings. Attempts at dissent or revolt were swiftly and ruthlessly squashed by the army and the rurales. Díaz also supported a countrywide system of *jefes políticos,* or local political bosses, who were loyal to him. The jefes políticos used threats, promises, and bullying to make sure that the common people did what the government wanted them to do.

The Mexican economy took a great leap forward during the Porfiriato. With the aid of a brilliant and earnest financial minister named José Ives Limantour, Díaz reorganized the country's troubled finances. To show that he was serious about economic reform, Díaz cut his own salary and the salaries of many government employees. He also ordered a crackdown on smuggling, which cost Mexico huge sums in lost import and export taxes each year. Limantour streamlined Mexico's income tax system and made the tax administration more efficient; he also managed to get loans from abroad. Eventually Limantour was able to repay some of the foreign debts and even to balance the national budget. In 1894, for the first time in Mexico's history, more money came into the country's treasury than went out of it. But the biggest economic success of the Porfiriato was a burst of growth and development that was based on foreign investments.

Díaz and the científicos went to great lengths to encourage foreign individuals and companies to invest their capital in Mexico. Díaz wined and dined visiting executives, and his ministers took them on tours of the country to show how peaceful and orderly Mexico had become. Díaz's government also arranged very favorable tax rates for investors, which made it cheaper for American and European companies to operate businesses in Mexico than in their own countries. As a result, foreign investment skyrocketed. Mines, ranches, ironworks and steelworks, and breweries were established by foreign investors. These investors not only built roads, railways, and telegraph lines to serve their businesses but also bought big stretches of land from the Mexican government. Foreign investors soon dominated Mexican business and industry, especially in the northern part of the country, where many huge mines and metalworking foundries were owned by American, French, and German millionaires.

All of this capital pouring into the country was like a reviving drink of water to Mexico's parched economy. Industry flourished. The amount of railroad track increased dramatically during the Porfiriato, from 400 miles in 1876 to 15,000 in 1911. Oil fields were discovered and quickly exploited by American and British companies—Mexico had large reserves of oil, and by the early 20th century it had become one of the world's major producers of petroleum. Old harbors at Veracruz and elsewhere were modernized to serve large new freighters, and new harbors were built along Mexico's Pacific coast.

Mexico City had a facelift, too. Drainage canals and tunnels were built to improve sanitation in the capital and prevent the constant threat of floods. The city also received new boulevards, parks, and statues, an electric streetcar system, and impressive public buildings ranging from a prison to a national theater. The capital hummed with a new sense of pride and enterprise, and all parts of the country reported that production was up in factories and farms.

Progress came at a heavy cost, however. The Pax Porfiriana *was* stable and orderly, but it was imposed by force and maintained by repression. Civil liberties, such as freedom of the press, were suspended. The government censored all publications. Any newspaper writer or editor who printed criticisms of Díaz was likely to end up in jail; one editor who campaigned against Díaz's seemingly endless string of re-elections was thrown in jail more than 30 times. Democracy itself was a casualty of the Porfiriato. Díaz threatened and bullied the members of congress until they were so obedient that he called the national legislature *"mi caballada,"* meaning "my herd of tame horses." As one rigged election or crooked vote count followed another, many people grew scornful and claimed that democracy could never work.

A caudillo himself, Díaz created a Mexico in which caudillismo prospered. Military rank was a shortcut to political power. By the mid-1880s a high percentage of state governors and legislators, as well as many of the 300 or more local jefes políticos, were military officers whose chief qualification for the positions they held was their loyalty to Díaz.

Land reform was set back many years by the Porfiriato. Many of the reforms that Juárez and others had tried to make were completely undone by new land laws. Under these laws, no peasant or farmer could claim to own his land unless he held a formal legal title to it, even if it had been his family's home for generations. Ejidos and small farmers were helpless—they could not afford lawyers to protect them against the land companies that gobbled up millions of acres of real estate along the new highway and railway routes and then sold the land to the hacendados. During Diaz's time in office, the large landowners gained even more land, and the *campesinos,* the small farmers of the countryside, lost what little they had. By the year 1910, all of the land in Mexico was owned by only 5 percent of the country's population. Díaz himself had given nearly one-fifth of Mexico's total area to his rich and powerful friends and supporters, both Mexicans and foreigners. Some of the hacendados possessed extraordinarily large empires. For example, the Terrazas-Creel family of Chihuahua, a state in northern Mexico, owned 50 haciendas and ranches totalling 7 million acres. They may have been the largest landholders in all of Latin America.

But very few Mexicans were hacendados. More than half of all rural Mexicans lived and worked as peons on the large haciendas, often in dirty and dangerous conditions. They were allowed to grow a bit of food

A MYSTERY MAN
AND HIS JUNGLE TALES

One of the most mysterious literary figures of the 20th century, the man who called himself "B. Traven," died in Mexico City in 1969. Although Traven published many books about life in Mexico, he kept his true identity a closely guarded secret. Many different versions of his life story appeared in newspapers and magazines; some of these false trails were laid by Traven himself to confuse people. At various times Traven was said to be a Norwegian fisherman, an American farmer, a Polish locksmith's apprentice, and the illegitimate son of the last emperor of Germany.

The riddle of B. Traven's life has not yet been fully unraveled, but German researcher Karl S. Guthke, author of a 1987 biography called *B. Traven: The Life Behind the Legends*, believes that Traven was really Ret Marut, a political activist who as a young man had tried to lead a revolution in southern Germany. Marut was sentenced to death in Germany in 1919, but he escaped and disappeared. Guthke thinks that he turned up a few years later in Mexico and began writing books under the name of Traven. A few of Traven's tales have international settings, but most are set in Mexico, a country that he came not only to love but also to understand. He had a keen eye for the details of everyday life as well as for the larger injustices of society, and he loved to roam the country and listen to campesinos and peons talk about their sorrows and joys, capturing the spirit of these encounters in his writing.

The question of Traven's identity still fascinates literary detectives, but his books stand on their own merits. The most famous is *The Treasure of the Sierra Madre*, the story of a desperate search for gold in the mountains of northern Mexico; it was made into a classic movie starring Humphrey Bogart. But Traven's favorite part of Mexico was the remote, jungle-covered south, especially the state of Chiapas on the Guatemala border. He spent months exploring Chiapas on horseback with a guide who had once been a peon in one of the region's notorious *monterías*, the lumber camps where thousands of laborers worked like slaves to harvest the valuable timber of the mahogany tree. Out of these journeys and Traven's own passion for social justice came his Jungle Novels, which were published between 1931 and 1940. Each of these books tells a simple story, but together they create a detailed portrait of how Mexico's poor lived and suffered during the Porfiriato. Set in Chiapas around 1910, the Jungle Novels are an epic of oppression and revolution.

The first book in the series is *Government*, the story of how a corrupt local official abuses the men he sends to work in the mahogany camps while he grows rich on their misery. The second book, *The Carreta*, is about Andres, who drives a *carreta*—an oxcart that carries freight across the mountains. Seeing how the rich and powerful exploit him and everyone around him, Andres becomes a revolutionary. The third book, *March to the Montería*, tells the story of Celso, an Indian youth who wants to earn money for his wedding. Celso is forced into the montería, but later he meets Andres and begins to rebel against the system. *March to the Montería* and the book that follows it, *The Rebellion of the Hanged*, describe the brutal life of the mahogany workers and the evils of debt peonage.

In *The Rebellion of the Hanged*, the Indian mahogany workers overthrow their bosses and escape through the jungle during the rainy season—an epic journey in itself. A spokesman for the rebels explains what they are looking for:

> We want land and liberty, and if we want that, we have to go and look for it where it is to be found and then fight for it every day to preserve it. We don't need anything else. If we have land and liberty we shall have all that man needs in this world, because it is in them that love is to be found.

The final book in the series, *General from the Jungle*, is set in 1910–11. It is the story of Juan Mendez, the leader of the desperate band of rebels from the montería, who wages guerrilla war against the soldiers of the dictator Porfirio Díaz. After the fall of the tyrant, Mendez finds a home in a village called Solipaz—its name means "sunlight and peace." The book ends with the triumphant cry, *"Tierra y Libertad!"* "Land and Liberty!"—the dream of Mexico's Indians and campesinos since Hidalgo's day.

for their families on small plots, but they had no chance to work these plots until after dark. They lived in shacks, and they had no medical care. On the worst haciendas more than one-fourth of all babies died before their first birthday, usually of diseases that could have been prevented with proper nutrition and sanitation. The peons' wages were tiny—and to make matters worse the wages were paid not in cash but in tokens that could only be used to purchase goods at the hacienda store, which was owned by the hacendado. Prices at these stores were very high, and the hacendados also charged the peons high rates for marriages, funerals, and festivals. The hacienda store system thus allowed the hacendado to make a profit on each of the peon's purchases, while at the same time it kept the peon continuously in debt and unable to break free. It was all but impossible for a peon and his family to pay off their debt to the hacendado, and peons who dared to run away were treated almost like runaway slaves and subjected to serious punishment if caught.

The Indians were the least-regarded part of Mexico's population during the Porfiriato. Many—though not all—of the científicos were racists who believed that the Indians were inferior to whites and could be governed only by force. This point of view was widely held among the criollos of the time; for this reason few criollos felt guilty about neglecting and overlooking the Indians. The Native American population reaped no benefits from Díaz's brave new Mexico.

The urban poor also suffered during the Porfiriato. Although the growth of industry created new jobs, drawing thousands of peasants from the countryside to the cities to seek work in the factories, working conditions were terrible. Laborers worked seven days a week, for 11 or 12 hours each day—children as young as eight or nine years old as well as adults. There were no labor unions, and few employers provided pensions for those employees who could no longer work because of age, illness, or injury.

The urban beautification spree under Díaz brought new statues and buildings to the better parts of town, but it did little to improve the lives of the masses. Great *barrios*—areas of slums and lower-class housing—sprang up on the fringes of Mexico City and other large cities. Life in these barrios was grim. Many people turned to alcohol and crime to enliven their dreary days. There was no indoor plumbing; one barrio in Mexico City had just one public bath house for every 15,000 people. Campesinos who flocked to the city for a chance at a better life found that the poor fared no better in the city than in the country. The average life span of a Mexican of the lower urban classes was about the same as that of a rural peasant: approximately 30 years.

Women made some strides forward during the Porfiriato, but there were large obstacles blocking women's rights and equality. Like other countries with a Spanish heritage, Mexico had long been a male-dominated society in which women had few independent rights. Nevertheless some upper-class criollo women were able to expand their horizons as the 19th century ended. The first woman graduated from Mexico City's medical school in 1887. Others became dentists, lawyers, writers, and professors. But the number of educated, professional women remained small, and some of the científicos sneered at them. When Laura Torres founded Mexico's first women's rights organization in 1904, a leading científico named Justo Sierra called it a club for old and ugly women.

Art is sometimes a form of rebellion, and a number of artists criticized Díaz's repressive regime and the inequalities of Mexican society. One of the most influential artists of the period was José Guadalupe Posada, whose black-and-white prints savagely illustrated the violence and greed that he saw just beneath the surface prosperity of the Porfiriato—for example, he portrayed a society lady as a grinning skull wearing a fashionable French hat. And a group of young artists, denied government funds for an art show because their paintings portrayed Indians and slums instead of the discreet landscapes favored by Díaz, proudly abandoned European artistic traditions to forge their own boldly Mexican style.

A century earlier, rebellious criollos had distanced themselves from the peninsulares by flaunting their American accents and using Indian words. Now, while Díaz, the científicos, and the wealthy elite slavishly followed French and Spanish styles in fashion and the arts, a handful of liberal artists and writers proclaimed their *mexicanidad,* or Mexican-ness, through their work. They painted and wrote about what they saw around them, not what European art academies and literary critics expected. Their work found only small audiences at first, but in years to come some of them would become internationally renowned.

As the Porfiriato wore on, more and more people spoke out against Díaz. Some of these were nothing more than rival caudillos, jealous of Díaz's long hold on power. But other uprisings showed that there was deep unrest within Mexican society. One important anti-Díaz action was a 1906 strike by workers in the large American-owned Cananea copper mine. Mine workers who were unhappy about their low wages and the lack of chances for promotion refused to let the mine operate until the owners listened to their grievances. The mine's managers ordered guards to fire on the workers, and several workers were killed. The riot spread to nearby communities, where workers broke into stores and stole guns and ammunition. With Díaz's permission, a troop of Arizona Rangers crossed the border from America and helped the rurales put down the strike by force. The ringleaders among the strikers were hanged; the other workers were disarmed and ordered back to work. The Cananea strike and the government's harsh response angered some thoughtful Mexicans who saw that Díaz was quicker to protect the property of foreigners than to help his own people.

A similar and even bloodier strike took place among textile workers the following year, when government troops killed at least 100 strikers. The strikes proved two things: that mass unrest was growing among the working class, and that Díaz would do anything to preserve the illusion that Mexico was an untroubled, peaceful place.

As the end of the 19th century approached, a growing number of liberal intellectuals insisted that the price Mexico was paying for progress was simply too high. They did not deny that the country was enjoying a boom in material prosperity, but they pointed out that that prosperity was ending up in the pockets of the wealthy and powerful few, while the many poor and powerless were in some ways worse off than ever before. People also criticized Díaz for turning so much of the country's land and resources over to foreigners, who now seemed much more important in Mexico than the ordinary Mexicans. There was also the question of law and democracy. Under Díaz, the liberties and freedoms for which Mexicans had fought and died ever since the time of Hidalgo had become a sham. Jefes políticos meted out justice in whatever way they pleased. No election could dislodge Díaz. The dictator was generally called Don Porfirio, a polite form of address that can be translated as "Sir

Porfirio," but some disgusted liberals took to calling him "Don Perpetuo" because he was perpetually re-elected.

By 1900 a small anti-Díaz movement was under way in Mexico. Liberal clubs formed in many communities, and several liberals managed to publish books that were highly critical of Díaz's policies. In August of that year three brothers named Jesus, Enrique, and Ricardo Flores Magón started a weekly liberal journal in Mexico City. They were thrown into prison for a year, but when they came out they found themselves heroes of the liberal movement; many intellectuals had joined the movement as a protest against Díaz's harsh treatment of the Flores Magóns. After two more arrests the brothers went into exile in the United States, but they continued to publish their journal. In 1904 they attacked Díaz in strong terms:

Forever—for as long as Mexico can remember—today's slavery will be identified with the name of the devil that made it all possible. His name is Porfirio Díaz, and his bestiality is being carried out in Mexico. . . . But the day of liberation is coming. Prepare yourselves my fellow citizens.

This article was nothing less than a call to revolution. The Flores Magóns and other exiled liberals soon settled in St. Louis, Missouri, and wrote their revolutionary plan. It called for the reinstatement of the Constitution of 1857, the restoration of ejido land to the Indians, the end of the hacienda store system, and a six-day workweek with workdays limited to eight hours. This plan showed that what had started as simple opposition to Díaz's constant re-elections had become a movement for true social reform.

To pay the costs of printing their journal, the Flores Magón brothers asked for help from liberals in Mexico. And they had received a cash donation from an unexpected source: Francisco I. Madero, the son of a rich hacendado in Coahuila state. Madero, who was educated in Paris and California, was more sympathetic than most landowners to the plight of the peons. He ran against Díaz's supporters in several local elections, but he soon realized that Díaz's jefes políticos controlled the vote. So he published a book that argued against presidential re-election and began touring the country, making speeches in favor of free elections.

At first Díaz and his cronies found Madero amusing. Madero was a small, quiet-voiced man, who did not eat meat or drink alcohol—the bluff generals in the Díaz government could not understand him at all. But then a liberal convention met and chose Madero to run for president in the election of 1910. Díaz was not happy to have a serious challenger in the 1910 election. That year, the 100th anniversary of the Grito de Dolores and Father Hidalgo's Revolt, was to be celebrated throughout the country as the centennial of the birth of Mexico's independence movement. Díaz had made elaborate plans for fireworks, parades, banquets, and other public displays. The last thing he wanted was a troublemaker calling attention to a crooked election. So when people started showing up at Madero's speeches and cheering him, the political machine lumbered into action. Madero was arrested. The Díaz regime spent 20 million pesos on the nationwide September 16 festivities—more than the country's education budget for that whole year, as historians Michael C. Meyer and William L. Sherman point out in *The Course of Mexican History*—but Madero missed the party. He was in jail.

Madero's family got him out of jail, and he slipped over the border into Texas. Unable to unseat Díaz in the voting booth, he decided that the time had come for rebellion. In the time-honored tradition of Mexican revolutionaries, Madero published a plan of principles and a call for action. Although he wrote it in San Antonio, Texas, Madero called his revolutionary document the Plan of San Luis Potosí after the city where he had been imprisoned. The Plan of San Luis Potosí was a declaration of war against Díaz and everything he stood for:

Fellow Citizens: If I call upon you to take arms and to overthrow the government of General Díaz, it is not only as a consequence of the excesses that he committed during the last elections, but also in order to save the nation from the somber future that awaits it if it continues under his dictatorship and under the . . . científicos who are unscrupulously absorbing and destroying the national wealth at great speed. . . . And because General Díaz intends to rely on brute force to impose an ignominious yoke on the people, they will have to resort to this same force in order to get rid of that yoke, to overthrow that doleful man from power, and to reconquer their liberty.

Mexico had seen many insurrections, coups, and rebellions, but what followed the Plan of San Luis Potosí was Revolution with a capital R. When history books refer to the Mexican Revolution, they mean the events that began when Madero urged all Mexicans to rise up against Díaz in November 1910. His call did not go unanswered. All over Mexico groups of rebels, ranging from upper-class liberals to rough-and-ready bandit chieftains, broke out in uprisings against Díaz. The rebel armies included many peons, but they also included teachers, factory and mine workers, street beggars and vendors, students, artists, criminals and bandits, and deserters from the federal army. The uprising was not merely a political revolt but a true social revolution. It drew together people from all ranks of society, and it carried the promise not just of legal elections and an end to the Porfiriato but of real social changes that would touch the life of every Mexican.

Leaders among the liberal intellectuals included Madero, the Flores Magón brothers, and a handful of lawyers and journalists. But three rebel leaders from humbler backgrounds quickly rose to prominence in the Revolution. In the north a large army gathered around a shop-keeper named Pascual Orozco and his friend Doroteo Arango, a cattle rustler and bandit who had changed his name to Francisco Villa and was usually called Pancho Villa. These two proved to be excellent military commanders. And south of Mexico City, in the mountainous state of Morelos, a farmer and horse trainer named Emiliano Zapata roused the local Indians against Díaz by making stirring speeches to them in their native language, Náhuatl. Zapata wanted to see Díaz overthrown, but his main goal was land reform, especially land for the Indians.

Over the years Díaz had faced many uprisings. He had always been able to control them without much trouble. This time, however, there were so many of them, happening so fast in so many different parts of the country, that he could not bring them under control. As soon as his troops had suppressed one outbreak of rebellion, another one would flare up somewhere else. Díaz was like a man slapping frantically at a whole swarm of stinging insects. The rebels were strongest in the northern province of Chihuahua. There Orozco commanded a large force that defeated a federal detachment in January 1911. After the battle Orozco stripped the bloodstained uniforms from some of the

Of all the rebel leaders who emerged during the Mexican Revolution, Emiliano Zapata was the most single-minded and honest. His one goal was to win land for the long-suffering Native American campesinos. (Library of Congress)

fallen federal soldiers and sent them to Díaz with a taunt that referred to *tamales,* a traditional Mexican dish of meat wrapped in corn husks—pinned to the uniforms was a note that read, "Here are the wrappers. Send me more tamales."

A few months later Orozco, Villa, and Madero captured Ciudad Juárez, a city on the northern border. The battle for the city raged for several days, while across the river in the American city of El Paso people climbed onto their roofs to cheer the side they favored, as though they were watching a football game. Eventually the federal garrison surrendered and the rebels took Ciudad Juárez. This victory was a turning point. Not only did it give the rebels control of the northern part of the country, but it prompted many federal soldiers to desert and join the rebel ranks. The country began to realize that the long Porfiriato was really coming to an end. The congress—Díaz's tame herd of horses—demanded his resignation. Mobs of *maderistas* marched on Díaz's national palace in Mexico City shouting, "Resign! Resign!" At one point Díaz ordered his guards to fire on the crowd, and 200 protestors were killed. But eventually Díaz had to admit that he was helpless. He resigned on May 25, 1911.

Díaz's resignation was greeted with with wild cheers from the maderistas. Edward I. Bell, an American who lived in Mexico City, later described the scene:

Within an hour the news had traveled to the furthest corner of the capital and the peones [sic] who had been quiet all day now mustered into line. There was management in this, not accident, not spontaneous movement, yet all was joy. By eight o'clock that night a monster parade wound through the capital streets. . . . Cheers for Madero rent the heavens. The revolution had won.

Madero came to Mexico City from the north by train. People lined the tracks to wave and cheer as his train passed, and in the capital he was followed everywhere by excited admirers. A 1917 book by Edith O'Shaughnessy, the wife of an American diplomat, describes how in 1911 the people adored Madero as though he were a saint: "People came from far and near, in all sort of conveyances or on foot, just to see him, to hear his voice, even to touch his garments for help and healing."

It seemed that the victory of Madero and the liberals was complete. Madero would be elected the next president, and he would set Mexico on the road to reform. The Revolution, it appeared, was over.

But in reality the Revolution had only gotten started. Some history books say that on his way out of Mexico the exiled Díaz remarked to General Victoriano Huerta, his military escort, "Madero has unleashed a tiger. Now let's see if he can control it." If this story is true, Díaz understood some aspects of the Revolution very well indeed. Madero was soon to discover that revolutionary Mexico was an immensely powerful force that he could not control at all.

CHAPTER EIGHT NOTES

p. 95   "We want land . . ." B. Traven, *The Rebellion of the Hanged* (New York: Hill & Want, 1952), p. 229.

p. 99   "Forever—for as long as Mexico . . ." Quoted in Michael C. Meyer and William Sherman, *The Course of Mexican History* (New York: Oxford University Press, 1991), pp. 485–486.

p. 100   "Fellow citizens: . . ." Francisco Madero, "Plan of San Luis Potosí." From *Revolution in Mexico: Years of Upheaval, 1910–1940*, ed. James W. Wilkie and Albert L. Michaels (Tucson: University of Arizona Press, 1969), p. 38.

p. 103   "Here are . . ." Meyer and Sherman, p. 502.

p. 103   "Within an hour . . ." Edward I. Bell, *The Political Shame of Mexico* (New York: McBride, Nast, 1914), pp. 82–83.

p. 103   "People came . . ." O'Shaughnessy, *Diplomatic Days*. Quoted in Meyer and Sherman, p. 506.

p. 104   "Madero has unleashed . . ." Meyer and Sherman, p. 511.

INDEPENDENCE AND REVOLUTION IN MEXICO

THE
CONSTITUTION
OF 1917

The Mexican Revolution was not a single event. It was a process that occurred in stages over a period of many years; in some ways it is still going on today. When Madero became president in 1911, the first phase of the Revolution ended, but the second phase began almost at once.

No sooner had Madero been sworn in as president than he discovered that there was little unity among the revolutionaries. His own goal had been to restore democracy in the form of honest elections and the rule of law. As far as broad social reforms were concerned, Madero felt that the country should progress slowly and carefully. Díaz had fallen, to be sure, but powerful conservative interests were still entrenched throughout the land. Madero feared that if the new revolutionary government pushed the conservatives *too* hard, they would fight back and perhaps regain control of the country. He therefore made only small gestures toward reforming education, land laws, and labor laws. He was supported by some of the liberal revolutionaries, who shared his view that change must be gradual.

But other revolutionaries—especially the peons and campesinos who had formed the bulk of the rebel army—expected Madero to bring about big, dramatic changes. They wanted a whole new social order, and they wanted it soon. They swiftly grew impatient with Madero's cautious, balanced approach to government, and before long open revolts had broken out.

Emiliano Zapata was the first to renounce Madero. Zapata was the most consistent of all the revolutionary leaders. From first to last, he had only one goal in view, and that was land reform for the Indians. He never wavered from that goal. He asked Madero to turn the large haciendas over to the Indians at once, and when Madero refused, he vowed that his army, the *zapatistas,* would continue to fight. Madero offered Zapata a fine hacienda of his own, hoping to keep the rebel leader quiet, but Zapata indignantly spurned the bribe. In November 1911 he announced his revolutionary plan, the Plan of Ayala, which declared that the Revolution should seize one-third of all large estates and give the land to the villages and people.

The zapatistas were strongest in Morelos and the nearby provinces but, as John Hart says in *Revolutionary Mexico: The Coming and Process of the Mexican Revolution,* their effect was felt throughout the country because their persistence encouraged other groups of Indians and mestizos to keep the Revolution alive:

Zapatismo was much more significant than the man and his immediate following in the south-central area of the nation. His revolution reflected a wider, grass-roots peasants' war.

The zapatistas formed themselves into units of local people, familiar with the terrain, who could make guerrilla attacks on both the federal army and the hacendados. They killed some hacendados and their families, and they drove the jefes políticos out of many communities. The ranks of the zapatistas included many women and children. Some officers were women—for example, a woman named Maria Chavarria held the rank of Coronela Zapatista, or colonel.

Women played a significant role in all of the revolutionary armies, not just Zapata's. Some served as spies or as smugglers of arms into Mexico from the United States. But thousands of them became *soldaderas,* or women soldiers, and marched with the armies. While some soldaderas came with the armies simply to cook and sew for their

Soldaderas, or women soldiers of the Revolution. Women fought in all of the revolutionary armies; their exploits were celebrated in songs and folk stories. (Library of Congress)

husbands or boyfriends, many others armed themselves and fought side-by-side with the men. They experienced the same uncertainties of war as the men—victories, defeats, long marches, and war wounds. The heroism of the soldaderas became the subject of many much-loved folk songs and stories.

While Zapata rebelled against Madero in Morelos, Pascual Orozco also rejected Madero in the north. Orozco's followers demanded reforms such as shorter workdays and laws to keep children from being exploited by employers. Moreover, Orozco criticized Madero for appointing more than a dozen of his own relatives to positions in the new government.

Not only did Madero face opposition from his former allies, but he had trouble with relatives of the exiled Díaz as well. Félix Díaz, the nephew of the former president, plotted a coup against Madero in February 1913. When fighting broke out in Mexico City, Madero made the mistake of turning the defense of the capital over to General Victoriano Huerta, who was both ambitious and callous. The episode that followed is called the *Decena Trágica,* the Tragic Ten Days.

For nine days Mexico City was a battleground for the forces of Huerta and Díaz, who sprayed the city with gunfire in their attempts to defeat each other. Buildings burned, stores were barricaded, and the panicked citizens huddled in their homes. The streets were empty save for looters. On the tenth day of fighting, Huerta switched sides. He and Díaz together took Madero prisoner. Díaz agreed to let Huerta become president, and Madero's dream of restoring democracy and open elections died. As for Madero, he and his vice president were killed, on Huerta's order or on Díaz's. The public was told that they had been shot "while trying to escape."

The Revolution had shifted into yet another phase. New battle lines were drawn, with Huerta and the federal army on one side and the *insurrectos,* or insurrectionists, on the other, led by Zapata, Villa, and Orozco. New insurrecto leaders emerged, too, drawn into the Revolution by their hatred of Huerta. Chief among these were Venustiano Carranza and Alvaro Obregón, each of whom would later serve as president. The insurrectos had many admirers in other countries. Men from the United States and Europe came to Mexico to offer their services to the Revolution. Some were ardent liberals who wanted to fight for freedom, others were mercenary soldiers seeking employment. Foreign journalists also traveled with the revolutionary armies and wrote about their exploits for newspapers around the world. One such journalist was the American John Reed, who a few years later would travel to Russia to witness the beginning of the communist revolution there. Reed rode with Pancho Villa's army and described his experiences with the insurrectos in his 1914 book *Insurgent Mexico.*

To combat the spreading Revolution, Huerta embarked on a repressive military dictatorship. He stopped at nothing to terrorize his opponents. On one occasion a senator named Belisario Domínguez stood up in congress and urged the legislature to throw Huerta out of office. "Mr. Victoriano Huerta is a bloody and ferocious soldier who assassinates without hesitation anyone who is an obstacle to his wishes," cried Domínguez. Two weeks later Domínguez was shot dead by an unknown assassin. When congress protested, Huerta closed both houses of congress and threw the congressmen into jail.

In one area Huerta did some good. The son of an Indian and a mestizo, he was fairly sympathetic to the plight of the Indians. His regime started a program to bring education into the Indian pueblos, and it also restored ownership of some ejido land to Indian villages. In addition, Huerta raised the taxes that the large landholders had to pay on their haciendas. In terms of social reform, in fact, Huerta's record was actually a bit better than Madero's, but the violence and tyranny of his rule reminded many people of the Porfiriato.

Huerta's downfall came in 1914. A minor quarrel between Mexican officials and American sailors in the Mexican port of Tampico blew up into an international incident when U.S. president Woodrow Wilson sent troops to occupy Veracruz. Deprived of the income from that port and beset on all sides by the insurrectos, Huerta was forced to resign. Once again the revolutionaries stepped into power—and once again a rift among them led to continued fighting.

The revolutionary leaders met in the town of Aguascalientes in October 1914 to choose a president and agree on a plan of action, but there was little agreement among them. Carranza, a former state governor, clearly expected to be chosen president, and Obregón backed Carranza. These two men were former maderistas who believed that reform should be gradual and orderly. But others at the meeting claimed that Villa and Zapata, who came from humbler backgrounds than Carranza and Obregón and who demanded rapid reform, were the true leaders of the Revolution. The villistas and zapatistas did not want to see control of the Revolution pass entirely into the hands of well-to-do criollo liberals. A zapatista named Antonio Díaz Soto y Gama asked what Carranza and Obregón planned to do for the Indians. "That which we called Independence was not independence for the Indian," Soto y Gama declared, "but independence for the criollo, for the heirs of the conquerors who continue infamously to abuse and cheat the oppressed Indian." More than 100 years after Hidalgo roused the Indians of Mexico to revolt with the promise of land, the question of rights for the Native Americans had at last moved squarely into the center of the country's political life. This issue would not easily be shoved aside again; it would keep returning to trouble all those who favored slow, moderate change.

After the arguments at Aguascalientes, the Revolution broke down into civil war between two opposing factions, with Carranza and Obregón on one side and Villa and Zapata on the other. Villa and Zapata

Mayo Indians from northern Mexico mustered with their traditional weapons to join the revolutionary army of Alvaro Obregón. These and other Native American revolutionaries were fighting for the return of their lands, which had been exploited for centuries by the Spanish and the criollos. (Library of Congress)

came face to face for the first and only time in Mexico City in December 1914. They agreed that men like Carranza would not help the poor campesinos. "Those are men who have always slept on soft pillows," Villa said. "How could they ever be friends of the people, who have spent their whole lives in nothing but suffering." Then Zapata went south to Morelos and resumed his war against the hacendados, and Villa turned north to battle Carranza's forces in the rugged highlands along the U.S. border.

The three years that followed Huerta's downfall were the most confusing era of the Revolution, with the country divided among as many as five rival governments at one time. No one group could establish overall authority. The differences between the various factions often became unclear, and some of the fighting had more to do with individual power struggles than with revolutionary ideals. Throughout this period Mexico's economy, as well as its relations with other nations, ground to a halt.

Perhaps the most famous—and certainly the bloodiest—battle of the Revolution took place in April 1915 at Celaya, northwest of Mexico

INDEPENDENCE AND REVOLUTION IN MEXICO

City. It pitted Villa, whose men were armed only with rifles, against Carranza, who had machine guns. Villa sent his army against Carranza's army again and again, only to be driven back each time. When Villa finally retreated, he left 4,000 dead on the battlefield, 5,000 wounded, and 6,000 taken prisoner by Carranza. After this defeat Villa's role in the Revolution changed. He became more of a bandit than a battlefield general. When President Wilson recognized Carranza's government as the legal government of Mexico, Villa turned against the United States and began raiding American ranches and towns. After the villistas attacked the town of Columbus, New Mexico, the United States sent 6,000 troops into northern Mexico to track Villa down and teach him a lesson. Led by General John H. Pershing, the Americans spent months combing dusty pueblos and dry valleys, but their search was in vain. They never found Villa, and everywhere they went they were greeted by scornful cries of *"¡Viva Villa!"* By the time Pershing and his men withdrew, their unsuccessful expedition had cost the U.S. government about $130 million.

Pancho Villa (center, wearing hat, on horse) galloped into history as a fiery revolutionary. His charisma captured the attention of people around the world, some of whom came to Mexico to fight at his side. After losing control of the Revolution, however, Villa became little more than a bandit. (Library of Congress)

By 1917 the civil war had claimed a million lives. Many of the victims were noncombatants who were killed in the pointless acts of violence that were committed by all sides in the conflict. Carranza, who had managed to strengthen his hold on Mexico City, decided that it was time to end the chaos that had engulfed the country and bring the Revolution into some kind of order again. He called a conference to draw up a new constitution. To avoid conflict, he excluded all villistas and zapatistas from the conference. Even so, his moderate position was outvoted by the radical members of the constitutional congress. The congress finally accepted a constitution that was based on the principles of social revolution, particularly the distribution of land to the peasants by the state and the right of workers to form unions and to strike. The Constitution of 1917 also limited the president to a single term; this provision was designed to give a president enough time in office to accomplish something but not enough time to become a dictator. In addition, the constitution was very strongly anti-clerical, severely limiting the role of the church in society. This anti-clericalism was to bear bitter fruit a few years later.

With the appearance of the Constitution of 1917, the Revolution entered yet another phase. For more than a century, radical reformers from Hidalgo through Zapata had fought for basic changes in the structure of Mexican society. Now those changes had become constitutional law, the very foundation of the state. But it remained to be seen whether the new constitution could truly transform Mexico.

CHAPTER NINE NOTES

p. 106   "Zapatismo was much more . . ." John Hart, *Revolutionary Mexico* (Berkeley, Calif.: University of California Press, 1987), p. 253.

p. 109   "That which we called Independence . . ." Michael C. Meyer and William Sherman, *The Course of Mexican History* (New York: Oxford University Press, 1991), p. 536.

p. 110   "Those are men . . ." Robert E. Quirk, *The Mexican Revolution, 1914-1915: The Convention of Aguascalientes* (New York: Citadel, 1963), p. 138.

THE CLIMAX OF
THE REVOLUTION

Venustiano Carranza was elected president in 1917. He promised to uphold the new constitution, but he believed it was much too radical, and once he was in office he failed to enforce it. He distributed only 450,000 acres of land to the ejidos instead of the millions that the reformers expected, and he did nothing to support workers' rights. Yet despite Carranza's dismal record as a reformer, a landmark in workers' rights took place during his presidency. In 1918 a labor leader named Luis Morones founded the country's first labor union. Morones later betrayed his cause by exploiting the union for personal gain; he flaunted diamond rings and drove imported Cadillacs, and he used thugs to force people to join the union. But his contribution was nevertheless an important one. Morones paved the way for workers all over Mexico to unite in the quest for better pay and conditions. Later union leaders avoided the pitfalls of corruption and helped the country's organized workers make remarkable progress toward fair treatment.

Emiliano Zapata, unshakable as ever in his determination to win land for the landless, rejected Carranza just as he had rejected Madero. In March 1919 he addressed a public letter to Carranza on behalf of the Indians who were still waiting for their land. Zapata accused the

President Alvaro Obregón (center) meets the Chinese ambassador to Mexico, the first foreign diplomat to recognize the Obregón government. Obregón's administration brought order and creativity to a nation that had been wracked by a decade of fighting. (Library of Congress)

president of using the Revolution as a stepping-stone to power. "It never occurred to you," wrote Zapata, "that the Revolution was fought for the benefit of the great masses, for the legions of the oppressed." Furious and embarrassed, Carranza decided to get rid of the troublesome Zapata once and for all. He arranged for one of his army officers to pretend to defect to the zapatistas—the pretender even killed several people to prove to Zapata that he was serious about switching sides. Then, when Zapata agreed to meet with the defector, the rebel leader was ambushed and assassinated. The officer who had carried out the plot was rewarded by Carranza with a promotion, and the Indians of Morelos—and of all Mexico—lost their most faithful champion.

But Carranza did not long enjoy his triumph. He met a similar fate just a year later. His former ally Alvaro Obregón mustered an army in revolt against Carranza and began marching toward Mexico City. Carranza fled the capital, only to be assassinated by one of his own soldiers as he tried to leave the country. Obregón became president in 1920. Thereafter the Revolution entered a calmer and more constructive phase as the fighting slowly diminished. Even Pancho Villa agreed to end his combination of banditry and guerrilla warfare. He settled down to retirement on a hacienda provided by the federal government. A few years later, in 1923, Villa too was assassinated, either by government agents or by private individuals seeking revenge for some offense he had committed. That same year a conservative revolt threatened to topple the Obregón government, but the federal forces brought it under control after a few months. The Constitution of 1917 remained in force, and Mexico was able, for the first time in years, to devote its attention to the economy and to civic life.

The Obregón era brought forth a burst of artistic activity, for the Revolution was a great source of inspiration for Mexican artists. Musicians were influenced by popular and traditional folk songs and marching songs, especially Indian melodies. Composers such as Manuel Ponce introduced a lively new mexicanidad to their music. Ponce used the *canción mexicana,* or Mexican song, as the pattern for his compositions. He wrote, "Amid the smoke and blood of battle were born the stirring revolutionary songs soon to be carried throughout the length and breadth of the land."

Novelists, too, found a compelling subject in the Revolution. In 1915 Mariano Azuela published *Los de abajo* (The Underdogs), which told the story of young man who is caught up in the Revolution, becomes a general, and is finally killed in the very spot where he had once ambushed some federal troops. Another important revolutionary book was Martín Luis Guzmán's *El águila y la serpiente* (The Eagle and the Serpent), published in 1928. It told of Guzmán's own experiences when, as a young man, he left the university to become a villista. Long after the fighting ended, the Revolution continued to nourish writers'

Muralist Diego Rivera painted this scene of land being distributed to the campesinos on a wall of the National Agricultural College in Chapingo. Land reform, a cherished ideal of Mexican revolutionaries since Miguel Hidalgo, began in earnest with the constitution of 1917. (Library of Congress)

imaginations. Carlos Fuentes, one of modern Mexico's foremost writers, was born in 1928, the year Guzmán's book was published. He did not experience the violent era of the Revolution firsthand, but he explored its meaning and effects in two novels, *The Death of Artemio Cruz* and *Where the Air Is Clear.*

But it was in painting that the Revolution really made its mark on the arts. Obregón's secretary of education, José Vasconcelos, hired young artists to decorate schools and public buildings with huge murals, or wall paintings, that depicted scenes from the Revolution or from Mexican history. The most important of these young artists were Diego Rivera, José Clemente Orozco, and David Sisqueiros, all of whom were active during the 1920s and 1930s. Their work glorified revolutionary ideals and gave heroic stature to the Indians and peons who had been overlooked for so long. The muralists gained international recognition—particularly Rivera, who also painted murals in the United States and Europe.

The Obregón regime made some progress in educational reform, thanks to Vasconcelos. More than 1,000 rural schools were built between 1920 and 1924, and traveling libraries were carried into remote pueblos and villages on muleback. In terms of land reform, Obregón distributed about 3 million acres of land to more than 600 villages, although the pace of reform was still too slow to satisfy the radicals.

Obregón was succeeded by Plutarco Elías Calles, a former teacher and governor from the northwestern state of Sonora. The 1924 election of Calles was the first time in 40 years that the transfer of power in Mexico had been accomplished peacefully and according to law instead of by fraud or force. It was hailed as the dawn of a new age of tranquility in Mexico. But Calles's presidency was soon disrupted by another furious revolt that divided the nation along lines of bitter opposition. Like the War of the Reform in the mid-19th century, the revolt of 1926–29 was about religion.

For nearly a decade the Catholic church had simmered with resentment against the anti-clerical Constitution of 1917. The priests, bishops, and archbishop grew angrier still when Calles set out to enforce the constitution's anti-clerical rules. These included provisions to the effect that religion could not be taught in schools, that priests had to register with the civil authorities, and that public worship outside a church was forbidden. All through Europe and the Americas, the age-old dominance of religion in public life was giving way to a new order in which the church had little or no power in government. Desperate to reverse this trend, or at least to hold on to what remained of its privileges, the Mexican church took an extreme step borrowed from the labor unions: It went on strike. Priests refused to celebrate Mass or to perform marriage, baptism, and funeral services.

The strike quickly mushroomed into an armed rebellion. Catholic leaders called upon the masses to support their church, and the people of Mexico—with a long tradition of devout Catholicism—answered the call. Soon federal troops were clashing with bands of Cristeros, as the pro-Catholic fighters called themselves. The conflict was fierce;

FRIDA KAHLO:
A VERY PRIVATE PAINTER

One of the greatest artists of the 20th century was a woman who lived through the Mexican Revolution but chose *not* to paint about it. Instead her subject was her own inner life of suffering, pride, and hope. In recent years she has become a heroine not just to other artists but also to Mexicans, who admire her national pride, and to feminists, who honor her for depicting a woman's life with fearless honesty.

Frida Kahlo was born in Mexico City in 1907 to a German father and a mestizo mother. Later Kahlo told people that she had been born in 1910; she was not trying to appear younger— she simply wanted to identify her birth with the dawn of the Mexican Revolution. Kahlo's life was haunted by misfortune. As a child she had polio and was bedridden for a long time. At the age of 15 she was the victim of a terrible traffic accident that smashed her spine and pelvis and left her with a legacy of lifelong pain. The accident made her an invalid for several years; throughout her life she underwent more than 30 operations as a result of it.

Kahlo began painting as a teenager. She had an easel attached to her sickbed, and she found an outlet for her emotions and her energy in art. Because she could not leave her bed in search of subjects to paint, most of her paintings were of herself, and searching self-portraits remained her specialty. She painted her own birth as well as gruesomely detailed scenes of her operations.

In the late 1920s she met the mural painter Diego Rivera, who admired her work, and the two were married in 1929. Unlike Rivera, who covered walls with huge paintings that celebrated

both sides committed atrocities and killed innocent civilians. The climax of the Cristero Rebellion came in 1928. Alvaro Obregón was elected to succeed Calles as president, but before Obregón could return to office he was publicly assassinated by a young man named

Mexican history or carried political and social messages, Kahlo explored her inner life on canvas. Her paintings were filled with images from her own life, yet they dealt with subjects that everyone knows: loneliness, life and death, and love.

Kahlo and Rivera led a tempestuous life. She was passionately devoted to him, but he was repeatedly unfaithful to her; in 1939 they were divorced. They remarried a year later and remained together until her death, although both of them had relationships with other people. Many of Kahlo's paintings from the 1930s and 1940s reveal the pain that her relationship with Rivera brought her—for example, in *The Heart* she painted herself with a hole in her body and her bleeding heart lying at her feet.

Mexicanidad, or Mexicanness, had been part of Kahlo's life since girlhood, when she defied fashion and began wearing the traditional braids and long skirts of the Mexican peasant woman. And although her paintings were personal rather than political, all of her works have a distinctively Mexican look. She used the style of Mexican folk art—simple shapes, bold colors, and clear outlines—rather than the more sophisticated techniques of European painters, and in her self-portraits she proudly exaggerated her Indian features.

In the 1940s Kahlo began to receive real recognition for her work. Her paintings were displayed in many museums, and she won several art prizes. At the same time, however, she was deteriorating physically. She had a series of operations on her spine, but her health steadily worsened and she became addicted to the painkilling drugs. In 1954, a year after the first one-woman show of her paintings, Kahlo died. The last entry in her diary read, "I hope the exit is joyful—and I hope I never come back. Frida."

Juan Toral, who turned out to be a fanatical Cristero. The trial of Toral and his accomplice, a nun called Madre Conchita, caused a public sensation. Toral was executed and Conchita was imprisoned. The assassin may have intended to strike a blow for the church, but his shocking act weakened public support for the Cristeros. A few months later the bishops and the government agreed on a compromise, and the churches reopened.

Calles could not succeed himself as president, so he chose a series of puppets to occupy the presidency until 1934. They took their orders from Calles, who thus continued to govern the country from behind the scenes. Calles took an important step in 1929 when he organized the Revolution into a formal political party with a structure and a set of rules. This new organization was called the National Revolutionary Party (PNR), and it dominated the political scene. The PNR has had several name changes over the years. Since 1946 it has been called the Institutional Revolutionary Party (PRI), but it is still the direct descendant of the Revolution of 1910 and the Constitution of 1917, and it continues to be the most powerful political party in Mexico.

To the dismay of the radical reformers in the party, the Revolution took a conservative turn during the second half of the Calles era. The compromise with the church was just one example. The pace of land reform slowed to a crawl after 1928, and some of the powerful hacendado families were allowed to buy back their former holdings. In 1934, however, things began to change again. A dynamic new figure swept into the presidency. His name was Lázaro Cárdenas. Calles expected the 29-year-old Cárdenas to be just another puppet, but he could not have been more wrong. Cárdenas turned out to be a true revolutionary president, one who restored the PNR to its progressive course and enforced the spirit of the 1917 constitution at last.

Cárdenas was from Michoacán state, west of the capital. His education had ended when he was 11 because his town had only an elementary school, but he had continued to teach himself by reading every book he could find. He became a newspaper reporter at the age of 16, and at 18 he joined the Revolution, eventually becoming governor of Michoacán. As governor he tried to live up to the ideals of the Revolution. He refused to line his own pockets with public funds, he listened respectfully to the grievances of Indians in his territory, and he even gave some land away to the peasants. His dedication to these principles did not waver when he became president. He refused to move into the lavish presidential mansion and instead lived in a modest style like any private citizen. He also continued to listen as gravely to factory workers and peasants as to government ministers and foreign dignitaries. A joke that circulated in Mexico City reveals Cárdenas's fondness for the common people:

One day the president's secretary brought him a list of urgent business and a telegram. The secretary read down the list. Agricultural production was down. "Tell the minister of agriculture," said Cárdenas. Railroads bankrupt. "Tell the minister of communications." Serious diplomatic message from Washington, D.C. "Tell the minister of foreign affairs." Then the secretary read the telegram. It said: My corn dried up, my burro died, my pig was stolen, my baby is sick. Signed, Pedro Juan, village of Huitzlipituzco. "Order the presidential train at once," said Cárdenas. "I am leaving for Huitzlipituzco."

Cárdenas achieved two major triumphs. The first involved the long-standing question of land reform. Determined to enact the constitution without further delay, Cárdenas gave away 49 million acres of land—from state holdings, land companies, and haciendas—to the peasant population. In contrast, all of the previous presidents had distributed a total of only 26 million acres. By the end of Cárdenas's term in office, a third of all Mexicans had received land.

Cárdenas gave the land not to individuals but to communities, in communal farms that were patterned after the Indian ejidos. The ejido system by no means solved all the problems connected with land ownership. Some campesinos wanted to own private land, and others complained that the ejidos were too small. Furthermore, people who had labored for decades as peons did not yet know how to organize themselves and work cooperatively for their own benefit, and the production of many of the ejidos was low at first. But despite these problems Cárdenas did more than anyone else to fulfill the promise that had been made to the Indians and peasants as long ago as Hidalgo's day.

Cárdenas's second triumph involved the oil industry, which had become Mexico's most profitable industry. The oil wells and refineries, although they operated on Mexican soil, were owned by foreign companies who paid Mexico taxes and a percentage of the profits—but most of the profits went to other countries. A growing number of Mexicans claimed that the oil companies should be nationalized, or brought under Mexican ownership. This notion was hotly opposed by the foreign nations, and when Cárdenas began to talk of nationalization companies such as Standard Oil urged the U.S. congress to make war on Mexico to protect its petroleum reserves. But Cárdenas, with a brilliant mixture of firmness and diplomacy, was able to negotiate a purchase price for the U.S. oil properties. The American companies demanded $200 million, Cárdenas offered $10 million, and the dispute was ultimately settled at $24 million. In 1938 the foreign-owned oil companies became the property of the Mexican state. From then on, Mexico would reap all the profits from its oil.

Cárdenas carried out other liberal reforms as well. He encouraged the growth of labor unions and allowed workers to take over some factories and businesses and run them cooperatively, like the ejidos. He also devoted more money to education than any earlier president and built many schools. He wanted to extend services to rural communities, and during his administration many villages received new bridges and running water. He also ordred rural hospitals to be built; money to run the hospitals was earned by state-owned movie theaters. Cárdenas also supported women's rights, and although the country was not yet ready to give women the vote in national elections, the president helped women's groups win the vote in a number of states. This paved the way for universal women's suffrage to be granted in the 1950s.

All in all, Cárdenas did his best to bring the Constitution of 1917 to life. He brought about real social change, change that was aimed at the betterment of *all* people, not just the privileged and powerful. Underlying Cárdenas's reforms was the belief that Mexican society, so long divided by race and class, could truly be unified. Cárdenas wanted the government and the people to enter into a new relationship. Instead of being constantly at odds, they would become one, and the state would speak with the voice of all its citizens. No longer would whole groups of the population be excluded from full participation in government. Unlike many presidents before him, Cárdenas made no attempt to cling to power after his lawful term of office was over. He retired gracefully into private life and continued to labor on behalf of the reform movement.

Cárdenas's presidency (1934–40) is viewed by many historians as the climax of the Mexican Revolution, the point at which the goals of people like Francisco Madero and Emiliano Zapata finally became reality. But Cárdenas's roots, like the roots of the Revolution itself, extend far back into colonial times. Cárdenas was the 20th-century successor to Miguel Hidalgo, who launched the reform movement with the Grito de Dolores in 1810.

CHAPTER TEN NOTES

p. 114   "It never occurred..." Michael C. Meyer and William Sherman, *The Course of Mexican History* (New York: Oxford University Press, 1991), p. 548.

p. 115   "Amid the smoke . . ." Robert Stevenson, *Music in Mexico: A Historical Survey* (New York: Crowell, 1971), p. 234.

p. 121   "One day . . ." Quoted in Anita Brenner, *The Wind that Swept Mexico: The History of the Mexican Revolution, 1910–1942* (Austin: University of Texas Press, 1971), p. 91.

MODERN MEXICO

Since Cárdenas's time, Mexico has experienced both victories and new troubles. Its government has been one of the most stable in Latin America. Mexico has suffered no more military coups, revolutions, or civil wars; nine presidents have taken office peacefully and served out their six-year terms. The stability that was longed for by leaders as different as Porfirio Díaz and Francisco Madero has arrived.

At the same time, however, civil unrest is still present in Mexico, and some segments of the population feel that the Institutional Revolutionary Party has let them down. The PRI has passed through many phases of liberalism and conservativism since 1940, and although the party is still based on the 1917 constitution, the revolutionary principles have not always been fully supported by those in power. In 1968 the International Olympic Games were held in Mexico City—this was the first time the Olympics had taken place in Latin America. But 1968 was also a year of student protests and radical political activity in many countries, and Mexico was no exception. Student riots broke out in Mexico City during the Olympics, and the federal authorities tried to quell them with a paramilitary riot-control force and later with the army, which only made the rioting worse. A bloody confrontation between protestors and army units left hundreds of students dead and made many Mexicans question the government's use of force to control dissent.

Since that time Mexico has not been free of human rights abuses. Human rights activists claim that opponents of the government have been arrested and jailed without trial, and that some of these political prisoners have been tortured; they also say that peasants in some districts have been terrorized by ultraconservative units within the army. There have been charges of serious political corruption as well. High-ranking officials have been accused of robbing the public treasury and taking bribes, and some army officers have been linked to the international drug trade, Mexico's largest law-enforcement problem.

Mexico faces two grave domestic problems: population growth and a troubled economy. Mexico has one of the fastest-growing populations in the world. In 1950 there were about 25 million people in the country; by 1992 there were more than 90 million. Mexico City alone grew from 3 million people in 1950 to more than 20 million in 1990—population experts consider it the world's fastest-growing city. But the city simply does not have enough jobs, housing, sewers, electricity, roads, schools, and hospitals for all those people. Rates of poverty, unemployment, and crime are increasing, and huge slums surround the capital. The country as a whole is equally ill-equipped to support a rapidly growing population. Malnutrition, illiteracy, unemployment, and poverty are still all too common across the country.

Most disappointing of all to the radical reformers, the gap between rich and poor has not closed very much in the years since the Revolution began. At the end of the 1980s, the poorest 20 percent of the population owned only 3 percent of the country's wealth, while the richest 20 percent of the people owned 54 percent of the wealth. Mexico's economy was boosted by high earnings from oil during the 1970s, but when world oil prices dropped in the 1980s the country's earnings dropped along with them. Inflation was high; in other words, the buying power of the peso kept slipping. By 1982 inflation was nearly 100 percent, which meant that over the course of the year prices for food and other consumer goods doubled—but people's incomes did not. Economic prospects have become so bad in Mexico, especially for the poor and uneducated, that each year thousands of Mexicans leave their country illegally to seek work in the United States.

On the other hand, many Mexicans now enjoy a far better life than their grandparents did. The 20th century has seen the growth of a middle class of educated professional people. Advances in medical care have touched many lives—the average Mexican now lives about 70 years, rather than 36 years as in 1930. And new loan and trade agreements with international banking organizations and with the United States offer some hope that Mexico's economy may revive in the years to come.

Mexico now occupies a far different place in the world than it did at the beginning of the 19th century. Then it was a colony, governed by the whim of the Spanish crown and exploited for Spain's benefit. Throughout the 19th century Mexico was absorbed in its own wars of independence and its struggle to define its national identity. Today, however, the country is a recognized participant in international affairs. At the end of World War II Mexico became one of the founding members of the United Nations, signalling Mexico's growing involvement in the world beyond its borders. In recent years Mexico has assumed a position of leadership among the nations of Latin America and also among the developing nations of the world—a role that would have astonished and delighted the 18th-century criollos who chafed under Spanish domination.

CHRONOLOGY

1519 • Spanish conquistador Hernán Cortés invades Mexico.

1535 • The Spanish colony of New Spain is created.

1552 • Bartolomé de Las Casas publishes *A Brief Relation of The Destruction of the Indies.*

1767 • The Bourbon rulers of Spain force the Jesuit religious order to withdraw from the Americas, angering the colonies.

1776–83 • Britain's North American colony wins independence in the Revolutionary War.

1789 • The French Revolution topples the monarchy of France.

1808 • A French army under Napoleon Bonaparte invades Spain; in Mexico, royalists stage a coup d'état against the viceroy.

1810 • Seeking Mexican independence and social reform, Father Miguel Hidalgo launches an insurrection against Spanish rule.

1811 • Hidalgo is executed by the royalists; José Morelos takes over leadership of the revolt.

1812 • Spanish liberals write a new constitution in Cádiz, Spain.

1813 • From Chilpancingo Morelos demands independence; from Apatzingán he issues a constitution.

1815 • Morelos is captured and executed.

1820 • A coup against King Ferdinand VII puts the liberals back in power in Spain; in Mexico, conservatives begin to favor independence.

1821 • Agustín de Iturbide, a former royalist army officer, joins the remaining rebels and brings down the viceregal administration. Mexico wins independence.

1822 • Iturbide is crowned Emperor Agustín I of Mexico.

1823 • Antonio López de Santa Anna leads a revolt against Iturbide, who steps down from the throne. Mexico becomes a republic.

1824–29 • Guadalupe Victoria is president.

1829 • A Spanish force attempts to recapture Mexico but is defeated by Santa Anna.

1831 • Vicente Guerrero is executed as a traitor.

1833–55 • The presidency changes hands 36 times. The average term of office is less than 8 months. Santa Anna serves as president 11 times. Several others serve three or more times.

1836 • Texas wins its independence from Mexico in a war that includes the siege of the Alamo.

1838 • The French attack Mexico to force repayment of debts; Santa Anna loses a leg in the "Pastry War," but his status as a national hero is cemented.

1846–48 • The United States invades Mexico in a territorial war. The 1848 Treaty of Guadalupe Hidalgo gives half of Mexico's territory to the United States.

1855 • Santa Anna's final term in power is ended by a liberal revolt, the Revolution of Ayutla.

1858–61 • During the War of the Reform, Mexico has two rival governments: conservatives in Mexico City and liberals, headed by Benito Juárez, in Veracruz.

1862 • The French invade Mexico.

1864 • The French make Archduke Maximilian of Austria the emperor of Mexico.

1867 • Liberal forces led by Juárez dethrone Maximilian. Juárez returns to the presidency.

1872 • Juárez dies in office.

1876–1911 • Porfirio Díaz governs as a dictator; he brings advances in industry and modernization, but human rights and liberal reforms suffer.

1910 • Francisco Madero, Pancho Villa, and Emiliano Zapata launch a revolution against Díaz.

1911 • Madero becomes president.

1913 • Madero is assassinated; Victoriano Huerta assumes power as a dictator.

1917 • The revolutionaries proclaim a new constitution.

1918 • Mexico's first labor union is formed.

1919 • Zapata is assassinated.

1923 • Villa is assassinated.

1926–29 • During the Cristero Rebellion, the church rebels against the loss of its traditional position in the state. Priests go on strike. Both pro-clerical and anti-clerical factions engage in violence.

1929 • The National Revolutionary Party (PNR) is formed and takes the dominant role in Mexican politics. (Today it is called the Institutional Revolutionary Party, or PRI.)

1934–40 • President Lázaro Cárdenas enacts many of the reforms promised by Hidalgo, Juárez, and the 1917 constitution.

GLOSSARY

alcalde   A mayor in colonial Mexico.

campesino   A rural person or country-dweller; never used to refer to wealthy landowners.

caudillismo   Rule by military chieftains; see *caudillo.*

caudillo   A leader—almost always from a military background—who rises to power by the force of a charismatic personality and the personal loyalty of his followers. Caudillos may be educated or uneducated, but they are always shrewd judges of public mood, exciting public speakers, and colorful, flamboyant individuals.

científico   Literally, a scientist or technologist. Used to refer to those among Porfirio Díaz's advisers who believed that scientific and technical progress were vitally important to Mexico's future.

corregidor   An officer of the crown who functioned as a district official in colonial Mexico.

coup d'état   (French for "blow against the state.") An attack upon a government from within.

criollo   A person of European descent who was born in the Americas; in Mexico, the criollos were descendants of Spaniards. Sometimes called creole.

ejido   A traditional landholding arrangement of the Indians in which a communal farm belongs to an entire village or community; the residents share the land, the work, and the produce.

---

encomienda A grant of land in Mexico awarded by the Spanish crown to the conquistadores and their descendants. The holders of the encomiendas were called *encomenderos,* and they had almost absolute power over the land and its native inhabitants.

gachupin A mildly insulting name used by criollos to refer to someone who had come to Mexico from Spain; also see *peninsular.* The literal meaning of the term is unknown.

gobernador A regional governor in colonial Mexico.

Grito de Dolores The "cry of Dolores"—Father Miguel Hidalgo's call for liberty that launched the war of independence in 1810.

guerrillero A guerrilla fighter; one who uses swift surprise attacks and stealthy retreats rather than open confrontation.

hacendado The owner of a *hacienda.*

hacienda A large rural estate, usually worked by peon labor. By the 19th century the term had replaced the earlier *latifundio.*

insurrecto An insurrectionist or rebel; specifically used to refer to the revolutionaries after 1910.

jefe político A political boss or chief, usually of a town or small region.

juárista A follower or supporter of liberal Benito Juárez.

junta A temporary or provisional government, usually a small committee.

latifundio A large farm or ranch.

lépero A beggar or outcast; the term was used primarily in Mexico City.

maderista A supporter of Francisco Madero.

mestizo A person of mixed white and Native American descent.

mexicanidad Mexicanness; a sense of identity as a Mexican.

mexicanismo Mexican nationalism; enthusiasm for Mexican history and culture. Similar to *mexicanidad* or Mexicanness.

milpa A family's small private garden plot.

moderado Someone with moderate views, whether liberal or conservative; someone who tries to reconcile opposing viewpoints.

patría Nationalism, or feelings of national pride and identity.

peninsular A person who came to Mexico from the peninsula of Spain, rather than being born in the colony, and whose loyalties lay with Spain rather than with Mexico. Also see *gachupin.*

Porfiriato The era of Porfirio Díaz's government (1876–1911).

---

puro A purist, or someone who insists on strict interpretation of an ideal; usually used to describe the liberals who were unwilling to compromise with the conservatives during the Reform era of the mid-19th century.

Reform The era in Mexican history that began with the Revolution of Ayutla in 1855 and lasted until 1872; during this time Mexico had two governments, one liberal and one conservative.

rurales Rural police force.

soldadera Woman soldier; used specifically for women who fought on the side of the revolutionaries after 1910.

villista A follower of revolutionary and bandit Pancho Villa.

zambo A person of mixed African and Native American descent.

zapatista A follower of revolutionary Emiliano Zapata.

FURTHER READING

ABOUT MEXICO AND ITS HISTORY

Anna, Timothy E., *The Mexican Empire of Iturbide* (Lincoln, Neb.: University of Nebraska Press, 1990). A scholarly survey of Mexican politics and government from 1821–61, with emphasis on the life and political career of Agustín de Iturbide.

———, *Spain and the Loss of America* (Lincoln, Neb.: University of Nebraska Press, 1983). A discussion of how the 1806–33 wars of independence in Spanish America—including Mexico—were related to events in Spain in those years.

Arrom, Silvia Marina, *The Women of Mexico City, 1790–1857* (Palo Alto, Calif.: Stanford University Press, 1985). Discusses the status and role of women, particularly criollos, from the end of the colonial era to the mid-19th century.

Bazant, Jan, *A Concise History of Mexico from Hidalgo to Cardenas, 1805–1940* (Cambridge: Cambridge University Press, 1977). Scholarly but readable; a good reference source for adults or advanced younger readers.

Bethell, Leslie, ed., *The Independence of Latin America* (New York: Cambridge University Press, 1987). A collection of brief, readable essays that survey the struggle for independence not just in Mexico but throughout Central and South America.

Casagrande, Louis B., *Focus on Mexico: Modern Life in an Ancient Land* (Minneapolis: Lerner, 1986). Written for young readers and illustrated with photographs, this book presents a look at life in Mexico today.

Fincher, E. B., *Mexico and the United States: Their Linked Destinies* (New York: Harper Junior Books, 1983). This illustrated book for young readers focuses on the relationship between Mexico and the United States and upon the images that people in each country have of the other.

Flores Caballero, Romeo, *Counterrevolution: The Role of the Spaniards in the Independence of Mexico, 1804–1838*, Jaime E. Rodriguez, trans. (Lincoln, Neb.: University of Nebraska Press, 1974). A history of Spain's control of the Mexico colony from 1540 to 1810, and an account of how Spain struggled to hold on to the colony during the wars for independence.

Green, Stanley C., *The Mexican Republic: The First Decade,1823–1832* (Pittsburgh: University of Pittsburgh Press, 1987). A scholarly history; very detailed but challenging reading.

Hamill, Hugh, *The Hidalgo Revolt: Prelude to Mexican Independence* (Gainesville, Fla.: University of Florida Press, 1966). Although not easy reading, this book gives one of the most complete looks at Miguel Hidalgo and the revolt he led.

Hart, John, *Revolutionary Mexico: The Coming and Process of the Mexican Revolution* (Berkeley, Calif.: University of California Press, 1987). This challenging but absorbing study presents the Revolution as a defense of Mexican independence, which was threatened by foreign interests; the Mexican Revolution is compared with revolutions in Russia and China.

Howard, John, *Mexico*, second edition (Englewood Cliffs, N.J.: Silver Burdett Press, 1991). An easy-to-read overview of Mexican geography, history and culture, illustrated with many photographs and designed for young readers.

Humboldt, Alexander von, *A Political Essay on the Kingdom of New Spain*, edited by Mary Maples Dunn (New York: Knopf, 1972). Originally published in 1811. Although its 19th-century style is not always easy to read, this lengthy book paints a vivid picture of colonial Mexican society on the eve of independence.

Humphreys, R. A. and John Lynch, *The Origins of the Latin American Revolutions, 1808–1826* (New York: Knopf, 1966). A collection of brief writings from scholars, freedom fighters, and diplomats, explaining why the people of colonial Spanish America rebelled against Spain's rule.

Irizarry, Carmen, *Passport to Mexico* (New York: Franklin Watts, 1987). A brief, illustrated description of Mexico for young readers.

Kandell, Jonathan, *La Capital: The Biography of Mexico City* (New York: Random House, 1988). Although long and very detailed, this book brings to colorful life the past and present of one of the world's major capitals.

Kurian, George, *Mexico and Latin America* (New York: Facts On File, 1990). A good reference source for information on the geography, population and economy of the region.

Martinez, Oscar J., *Fragments of the Mexican Revolution: Personal Accounts from the Border* (Albuquerque: University of New Mexico Press, 1983). The Mexican Revolution as seen through the eyes of its American neighbors.

Meyer, Michael C. and William Sherman, *The Course of Mexican History* (New York: Oxford University Press, 1991). A first-rate overview of Mexico from ancient times through the 1980s; a good reference source.

Miller, Robert Ryal, *Mexico: A History* (Norman, Okla.: University of Oklahoma Press, 1985). Covers Mexico's history from before the Spanish conquest to the present; detailed and challenging reading, but with many colorful anecdotes.

Olivera, Ruth and Liliane Crete, *Life in Mexico under Santa Anna, 1822–1855* (Norman, Okla.: University of Oklahoma Press, 1991). Uses quotes from many 19th-century diaries, histories and travel books to paint a picture of social life, education, entertainment and customs among all classes.

Oster, Patrick, *The Mexicans: The Personal Portrait of a People* (New York: Morrow, 1989). A journalist's study of the Mexican national character and of Mexico's social order and political and economic life; portraits of real people from all walks of life.

Paz, Octavio, *The Labyrinth of Solitude: Life and Thought in Mexico,* Lysander Kemp, trans. (New York: Grove, 1961). A study of the Mexican character by one of 20th-century Mexico's leading poets and philosophers.

Pendle, George, *A History of Latin America* (New York: Penguin, 1987). First edition 1963. An unusually brief and readable overview of events in Mexico and Central and South America from before the conquistadores to the present; a good choice for the student who wants a broad picture in less than 250 pages.

Perl, Lila, *Mexico: Crucible of the Americas* (New York: Morrow, 1978). An illustrated overview of Mexico's geography, history, economy and culture for young readers.

Reavis, Dick J., *Conversations with Moctezuma: Ancient Shadows over Modern Life in Mexico* (New York: Morrow, 1990). A personal account by a journalist who lived and traveled in Mexico, talking to a variety of people and exploring the links between the country's history and life there today.

Reed, John, *Insurgent Mexico* (New York: Appleton, 1914. Reissued by Simon & Schuster, 1969). Personal and vivid descriptions of the Mexican Revolution, the soldaderas, the villistas, and more by an American journalist who rode with Pancho Villa.

Richmond, Douglas, ed., *Essays on the Mexican War* (College Station, Tex.: Texas A & M Press, 1986). A collection of scholarly papers about various aspects of the 1846–48 war; challenging but informative reading.

Riding, Alan, *Distant Neighbors: Portrait of the Mexicans* (New York: Knopf, 1984). A survey of Mexican society, politics and economy; the author's starting point is, "Probably nowhere in the world do two countries as different as Mexico and the United States live side by side. . . . Probably nowhere in the world do two countries understand each other so little."

Robertson, William Spence, *Rise of the Spanish-American Republics As Told in the Lives of Their Liberators* (New York: Collier, 1961).

Short but detailed biographies of seven men who fought in the Spanish-American wars of independence, including Miguel Hidalgo and Agustín de Iturbide of Mexico.

Rodman, Selden, *A Short History of Mexico* (New York: Stein & Day, 1982). A colorful description of Mexican history as a guide to travel in Mexico, by a travel writer and critic of art and music.

Rummel, Jack, *Mexico* (New York: Chelsea House, 1990). For junior high and high school readers, an overview of Mexico's geography, culture and history; includes a map and numerous illustrations.

Simpson, Lesley Byrd, *Many Mexicos*, fourth edition (Berkeley, Calif.: University of California Press, 1966). This classic volume interprets Mexico's history from a conservative point of view, with many anecdotes and details that make for lively reading.

Stein, Conrad, *Mexico* (Chicago: Childrens Press, 1984). For young readers; an illustrated overview of Mexican geography, history, economy and culture.

Wilkie, James W. and Albert L. Michaels, eds., *Revolution in Mexico: Years of Upheaval, 1910–1940* (Tucson: University of Arizona Press, 1969). A collection of excerpts from documents by and about revolutionary leaders; includes Madero's Plan of San Luis Potosí as well as firsthand descriptions of Villa and Zapata.

BIOGRAPHIES

Jones, Oakah L., Jr., *Santa Anna* (New York: Twayne, 1968). A very readable biography by the author of several books on Mexican affairs.

Lieberman, Mark, *Hidalgo: Mexican Revolutionary* (New York: Praeger, 1970). One of the few full-length biographies of Hidalgo; gives a good account of the revolt.

Ragan, John D., *Emiliano Zapata* (New York: Chelsea House, 1989). A biography for young adult readers that places Zapata's revolutionary career in the context of his times.

Robertson, William Spence, *Iturbide of Mexico* (Durham, N.C.: Duke University Press, 1962). A scholarly and detailed biography of Mexico's first emperor; challenging reading.

Rouverol, Jean, *Juárez: A Son of the People* (New York: Crowell-Collier, 1973). Written for young readers; tells the story of the Zapotec Indian who led Mexico into an era of reforms.

————, *Pancho Villa: A Biography* (Garden City, N.Y.: Doubleday, 1972). A biography of the bandit-revolutionary written for young readers.

Syme, Ronald, *Zapata: Mexican Rebel* (New York: Morrow, 1971). A short and easy-to-read biography for young readers.

Santa Anna, Antonio López de, *The Autobiography of Santa Anna*, translated by Sam Guyler and Jaime Platon; edited by Ann Fears Crawford (Austin, Tex.: Pemberton, 1967). Santa Anna's own version of his life story, filled with entertaining—but unreliable—accounts of his cleverness and bravery.

Smart, Charles A., *Viva Juárez!* (Philadelphia: Lippincott, 1963). A lengthy biography, written for adults and advanced younger readers.

Von Hagen, Victor W., *Search for the Maya: The Story of Stephens and Catherwood* (New York: Gordon & Cremonesi, 1973). A very readable account of several historic expeditions to uncover Maya ruins in the years 1839–41.

Wepman, Dennis, *Benito Juárez* (New York: Chelsea House, 1986). A biography for young adult readers; focuses on Juárez's struggle to win rights for the Indians and other oppressed Mexicans.

Womack, John, *Zapata and the Mexican Revolution* (New York: Knopf, 1968). Covers not just Zapata's life but also the course of the Revolution after his death.

ABOUT MEXICAN ART AND LITERATURE

Cockcroft, James, *Diego Rivera* (New York: Chelsea House, 1991). Written for junior high and high school readers; covers Rivera's life and political activities as well as providing an introduction to his painting.

Drucker, Malka, *Frida Kahlo: Torment and Triumph in Her Life and Work* (New York: Bantam, 1991). A biography that focuses on the many tragedies and difficulties of Kahlo's life and how they shaped her paintings.

Goldman, Shifra M., *Contemporary Mexican Painting in a Time of Change* (Austin, Tex.: University of Texas Press, 1981). A survey of 20th-century Mexican painting, with emphasis on the large murals of Rivera and other revolutionary artists.

Guthke, Karl S., *B. Traven: The Life Behind the Legends*, Robert C. Sprung, trans. (Brooklyn: Lawrence Hill, 1991). An attempt to solve the mystery of the identity of B. Traven, the reclusive novelist who wrote tales of life in Mexico.

Herrera, Hayden, *Frida: A Biography of Frida Kahlo* (New York: Harper & Row, 1983). The major book about an artist whose work has been increasingly prized since the early 1980s.

Paz, Octavio, *Sor Juana: Or, the Traps of Faith*, translated by Margaret Sayers Peden (Cambridge, Mass.: Harvard University Press, 1988). One of Mexico's most important 20th-century writers describes the life and works of the country's greatest colonial poet.

Rivera, Diego, *The Murals of Diego Rivera* (London: Journeyman, 1987). A collection of Rivera's murals, most of which depict revolutionary themes.

Robinson, Cecil, ed. and trans., *The View from Chapultepec: Mexican Writers on the Mexican-American War* (Tucson: University of Arizona Press, 1979). Reviews attitudes and public opinion in Mexico during the 1846–48 war; presents the war from Mexico's point of view.

Rojas, Pedro, *The Art and Architecture of Mexico*, J. M. Cohen, trans. (Feltham, England: Hamlyn, 1968). An illustrated survey of Mexican art and architecture from ancient times.

Rutherford, John, *An Annotated Bibliography of the Novels of the Mexican Revolution of 1910–1917* (Troy, N.Y.: Whitston, 1972). For readers who want to read fiction written about the Revolution, this book lists and describes novels with revolutionary subjects.

Tyler, Ron, ed., *Posada's Mexico* (Washington, D.C.: Library of Congress, 1979). A guide to the illustrations of José Guadalupe Posada, whose dark visions of life under the dictatorship of Porfirio Díaz inspired Rivera and other revolutionary artists.

FICTION

Azuela, Mariano, *The Underdogs,* E. Munguia, trans. (New York: New American Library, 1963). A novel of social criticism that follows the adventures of a revolutionary; first published in 1915.

Fuentes, Carlos, *The Death of Artemio Cruz,* Sam Hileman, trans. (New York: Farrar, Straus & Giroux, 1964). A novel about the Revolution by one of modern Mexico's foremost contemporary novelists.

———, *Where the Air Is Clear,* Sam Hileman, trans. (New York: Farrar, Straus & Giroux, 1960). A novel about life after the Revolution; it deals with the themes of power, corruption, and the difficulty of building a better world with imperfect human beings.

Guzmán, Martín Luis, *The Eagle and the Serpent,* Harriet Onis, trans. (New York: Dolphin, 1965). The memoir of a university student who joined the Revolution and fought with Pancho Villa; Guzmán is famous for having described the Revolution as a "fiesta of blood."

Traven, B., *The Carreta* (New York: Hill and Wang, 1970). The second of the author's Jungle Novels, which describe the lives of downtrodden peons in southern Mexico and tell how they became revolutionaries.

———, *The General from the Jungle* (New York: Hill and Wang, 1970). The fifth in the Jungle series.

———, *Government* (New York: Hill and Wang, 1971). The first in the Jungle series.

———, *March to the Montería* (New York: Hill and Wang, 1971). The third in the Jungle series.

———, *The Rebellion of the Hanged* (New York: Hill and Wang, 1972). The fourth in the Jungle series.

———, *The Treasure of the Sierra Madre* (New York: Pocket Books, 1961). The story of a desperate treasure hunt in strife-torn northern Mexico.

INDEX

Boldface numbers indicate major topics.
Italic numbers indicate illustrations.
Numbers followed by "m" indicate maps.

Declaration of Independence 13
Díaz, Félix 107–108
Díaz, Porfirio
 dictatorship 89–93, 96–103, 129
 fall from power 103–104
 military career 82
 portrait *90*
 president 89
Díaz del Castillo, Bernal 32
Dolores 19, 20
Domínguez, Belisario 108
Dominicans 9
drug traffic 125
Durango 84

Eagle and the Serpent, The See El águila y la serpiente 115
economy *See also* trade
 colonial 10–11, 19, 45
 foreign investment 90, 92
 growth of 89–92
 and independence 44–45, 47
 prospects 126
 and Revolution 110
education 85–86, 117, 122
ejidos 50, 86, 93, 109, 121, 130
El Paso 103
El Salvador 46
Elizondo, Ignacio 25
emigration 125
encomiendas 4–5, 9, 131
Enlightenment 14
Europe *See name of country*

Father Hidalgo *See* Hidalgo y Costilla, Miguel

Ferdinand VII, king of Spain 18, 22, 34–35, 37–38, 42, 82, 127
Ferdinand Maximilian, archduke of Austria *See* Maximilian I
Fernández, Manuel Félix
 See Victoria, Guadalupe
Flores Magón brothers 99
France 66–67, 81–84, 128, 129
Franciscans 9
French Revolution 13–14, 15, 127
Fuentes, Carlos 116

gachupines 11, 15, 35, 131 *See also* peninsulares
Galván, Rodríguez 58
geography 1, 2–4
gobernadores 2, 131
gold rush 72
Goliad 65
Gómez Farías, Valentin 57, 60, 64
Gómez Pedraza, Manuel 55, 56
Gonzalez, Manuel 89
Grito de Dolores 21, 27, 100, 131
Guadalajara 24, 80, 84
Guanajuato 22–23, 25, 59
Guatemala 3, 46, **68**
Guerrero, Vicente 29, 34, 38, 39, 44, 47–48, 55–56, 128
guerrilla warfare 29, 83, 106 *See also* guerrilleros
guerrilleros 29, 131
Gulf of Mexico 1, 34
Guzmán, Martin Luís 115

hacendados 86, 93, 131
haciendas 86, 131
Hapsburgs 12
Hart, John 106